D1564486

Activist Rhetorics and American Higher Education
1885–1937

ACTIVIST RHETORICS AND AMERICAN HIGHER EDUCATION 1885–1937

Susan Kates

Southern Illinois University Press
Carbondale and Edwardsville

Library of Congress Cataloging-in-Publication Data
Kates, Susan, 1961–
    Activist rhetorics and American higher education, 1885–1937 / Susan Kates.
        p. cm.
    Includes bibliographical references and index.
    1. English language—Rhetoric—Study and teaching—United States—History—20th
century. 2. English language—Rhetoric—Study and teaching—United States—
History—19th century. 3. English language—Rhetoric—Study and teaching—Social
aspects—United States. 4. Report writing—Study and teaching (Higher)—United
States—History—20th century. 5. Report writing—Study and teaching (Higher)—
United States—History—19th century. 6. Alternative education—United States—
History—19th century. 7. Alternative education—United States—History—20th
century. 8. Minorities—Education (Higher)—United States—History. 9. Women—
Education (Higher)—United States—History. I. Title.
PE1405.U6 K38 2001
808'.042'071173—dc21
ISBN 0-8093-2340-0 (cloth : alk. paper)   00-020817

The paper used in this publication meets the minimum requirements of American
National Standard for Information Sciences—Permanence of Paper for Printed Library
Materials, ANSI Z39.48-1992. ♾

To Frank

Contents

Illustrations

Preface

Activist Rhetorics and American Higher Education, 1885–1937 is a history of the rhetorical instruction generated by educators who taught at three institutions founded to serve middle-class white women, African Americans, and workers in late-nineteenth- and early-twentieth-century America. A central goal of this work is to provide a detailed overview of the curricula produced by Mary Augusta Jordan of Smith College, Hallie Quinn Brown of Wilberforce University, and Josephine Colby, Helen Norton, and Louis Budenz of Brookwood Labor College. I argue that because of the commitment of these teachers to students who were often denied admission to the more elite institutions on the basis of their gender, race, or social class, they created a course of rhetorical study designed to confront the sexism, racism, and classism in the larger culture through a curriculum defined by its politics of difference.

My aim in writing a history of rhetoric courses designed for disenfranchised students of other times is to demonstrate that many of the present issues with which we struggle have faced rhetoric teachers in other historical moments. In an era when multiculturalism has become the educational buzz word, few have looked to the past to ask how history might inform our theory and our practice as we consider how to create more equitable educational opportunities for students. We would do well to remember that we are not the first generation of educators to suggest that rhetoric instruction is ideological and certainly not the first to emphasize the features of what I call *activist education*—by this term I mean rhetorical study that pursues the relationship between language and identity, makes civic issues a theme in the rhetoric classroom, and emphasizes the responsibility of community service as part of the writing and speaking curriculum. I argue that an activist rhetoric instruction is, in many ways, the predecessor of what we have more recently come to call *critical pedagogy*. Critical pedagogy gained recognition in the 1960s and 1970s through the work of Paulo Freire and his literacy efforts with Brazilian peasants; since then, efforts to translate the social and ethical goals of critical pedagogy in the United States have been widespread. This book demonstrates that many of the aims of critical education outlined by Freire and others were envisioned and enacted long before the second half of the twentieth century and are evident in the pedagogical legacies left to us by Jordan, Brown, Colby, Norton, and Budenz.

While the history of rhetoric and composition in nineteenth- and twentieth-century America is a rich one, it is a history that we have only recently begun to write. Even broad examinations of nineteenth- and twentieth-century rhetoric courses in America offer very little information about separatist institutions that were founded to serve students who could seldom gain access to more elite colleges and universities. My project, although it is certainly a localized view, begins to address a gap in our discipline. I argue that we will not have an accurate portrait of rhetorical instruction in America nor will we implement the tenets of multiculturalism and critical pedagogy effectively until we better understand how diverse groups of Americans studied rhetoric in other times in courses defined by their activism. The pedagogical responses of these educators demonstrate that whether we call it "critical pedagogy," "activist rhetorical instruction," or "multicultural education," generating curricula for diverse student populations is never an easy task.

This history spans the years 1885—when Jordan first joined the faculty at Smith College—to 1937—when Brookwood Labor College closed its doors. In constructing this work, I have attempted to account for the social and political forces that shaped the curriculum design of these rhetoric teachers. In other words, I examine events within women's history, African American history, and labor history and their influence on rhetorical study as it was conceived by those educators who directed their courses toward very specific groups of students. I take up, for example, the issues of suffrage and coeducation and their influence on topics of debate in women's colleges in the late nineteenth and early twentieth centuries; I examine the effects of racism on the formation of black colleges and universities; and I provide an overview of the climate that inspired the labor movement to enact workers' education in the 1920s and 1930s. It is my hope that this overview demonstrates how the disenfranchisement experienced by these groups of students necessitated the founding of academic institutions that could address their ill-treatment in the larger culture.

I have consulted a wide variety of archival materials that include student papers, college mission statements, correspondence from students and teachers, and newspaper articles about these educators and their respective institutions, as well as articles written by the pedagogical architects in this study. In this respect, my work moves beyond simple textbook historiography to present a detailed and complex portrait of activist rhetoric instruction as it was crafted and enacted by these educators. My method of historiography owes much to other rhetoric historians who take up pedagogical history to improve contemporary praxis. I am particularly indebted to James Berlin's *Writing Instruction in Nineteenth-Century American Colleges* and *Rhetoric and Reality: Writing Instruction in American Colleges, 1900–1985* for the overview these texts provide of rhetoric instruction that functions to serve present pedagogical concerns. My work also aspires to the level of curricular detail provided in Robin Varnum's *Fencing with Words*, which examines the history of English 1-2 at Amherst College, where Theodore Baird directed writing courses from 1938 to 1966. Varnum's text provides the kind of close examination of rhetorical instruction at one institution that has seldom been the focus of pedagogical histories. In it, she allows us to understand the ideological aims of the liberal education of the time and the ways in which Baird's intellectual politics helped to shape the teaching of the course.

My history differs from Berlin's, Varnum's, and others', however, in terms of its focus on particular student constituencies and the ways in which their marginalization in the larger culture became a focus of the course content, forming the basis for assignments that asked them to interrogate their status and that of other members of their community. I examine both writing and speaking courses in this study because I am interested in pedagogical artifacts that correspond to the features of activist rhetoric instruction—a course of study defined by its attention to language and the philosophical issues that surround it. In every case, these rhetoric teachers generated pedagogical materials that went beyond a superficial concern for correctness and asked students to think about language in complex and, I would argue, ideological ways.

The chronology of these sites moves from the least radical—from Smith College, where the mode of politicization of the rhetoric course is more subversive—to the most radical—Brookwood Labor College, where the mission statement and other documents clearly and overtly articulate the ideological aims of workers' education. In many cases, the instruction these teachers extended to students was often "extracurricular"; that is to say, it reached beyond their respective institutions to students outside the academic institutions in which they taught. Jordan wrote a rhetoric textbook to be used by members of white women's clubs. Brown composed pedagogical materials and edited a reciter text that, like many other reciter texts published in its day, often became a fixture in the homes of African Americans who would never attend any college or university. Colby, Norton, and Budenz authored pamphlets that were used in workers' education classes across the country. Of all the pedagogies of these educators, Hallie Quinn Brown's is the most "extracurricular" in its treatment of elocutionary practice designed for African American audiences outside the formal academy.

I argue throughout this book that those of us committed to making the university a place that honors the increasingly diverse student population of the country must invoke history to do that work. Though much of the history examined here may not translate directly to our own context because of the separatist nature of the schools for which these curricula were designed, an examination of the goals and enactments of these forms of rhetorical instruction have much to teach us about how to continue the project of democratizing education in the twenty-first century. While I would emphasize that these pedagogical models do not provide exact blueprints for us, they do speak to the efforts to create equitable rhetoric curricula and the challenges that must be faced in doing so. Above all, it is my hope that the struggles and achievements of these activist educators will inspire us to extend their goals through our own contributions to this ongoing history.

Acknowledgments

No book is ever the work of one individual; I am most grateful for the financial and intellectual support I have received from a variety of institutions and people. Ohio State University and the University of Oklahoma provided me with grants of funds that enabled me to travel to archives to study and collect materials. Thanks go to archivists Maida Goodwin and Margery Sly at Smith College, Isabel Jasper at the National Afro-American Museum, George Johnson at Central State University, and Thomas Featherstone at the Walter P. Reuther Library at Wayne State University for their assistance throughout my work on this project.

I owe a tremendous debt to colleagues and friends who read this manuscript with great care. Cheryl Glenn, Amy Goodburn, Karyn Hollis, Andrea Lunsford, Sue Carter Simmons, Shirley Wilson Logan, and Warren Van Tine nurtured this book in very important ways, providing me with new ideas and valuable sources of information. I am grateful to Michael Flanigan, Catherine Hobbs, David Mair, and Kathleen Welch in the composition, rhetoric, and literacy program at the University of Oklahoma who offered me their feedback and support. Thanks go as well to other generous colleagues in and out of the English department: Daniel Cottom, Robert Murray Davis, Julia Ehrhardt, Larry Frank, David Gross, Catherine John, Susan Laird, David Levy, and especially Ronald Schleifer for the time and energy they devoted to this manuscript.

I also express heartfelt thanks to my family who encouraged me throughout my research and writing. Finally, the dedication of this book acknowledges the immeasurable support of my husband, Frank, who did so much to make the writing possible.

Earlier versions of portions of chapters 2 and 3 were previously published as follows: "Subversive Feminism: The Politics of Correctness in Mary

Augusta Jordan's *Correct Writing and Speaking* (1904)," *College Composition and Communication* 48 (December 1997): 501–17; and "The Embodied Rhetoric of Hallie Quinn Brown," *College English* 59 (January 1997): 59–71.

ACTIVIST RHETORICS AND AMERICAN HIGHER EDUCATION 1885-1937

1

EDUCATIONAL POLITICS: RHETORICAL INSTRUCTION AND THE DISENFRANCHISED STUDENT

> One cannot expect positive results from an educational or political action program which fails to respect the particular view of the world held by the people. Such a program constitutes cultural invasion, good intentions notwithstanding.
> —Paulo Freire, *Pedagogy of the Oppressed*

This book examines the forms of activist rhetoric instruction that emerged for three particular groups of students that were most often excluded from traditional institutions of higher education in America: white women, African Americans, and members of the working class. It explores the pedagogies of educators affiliated with three specific academic institutions founded to serve these groups of students: Mary Augusta Jordan of Smith College, in Northampton, Massachusetts; Hallie Quinn Brown of Wilberforce University, in Wilberforce, Ohio; and Josephine Colby, Helen Norton, and Louis Budenz of Brookwood Labor College, in Katonah, New York. At these locations, educators taught writing and speaking courses that diverged in significant ways from those offered at more traditional institutions. In their efforts to educate particular student constituencies and enact forms of writing and speaking instruction that incorporated social and political concerns in the very essence of their pedagogies, the teachers in this study designed rhetoric courses characterized by three important pedagogical features: (1) a profound respect for and awareness of the relationship between language and identity and a desire to integrate this awareness into the curriculum; (2) politicized writing and speaking assignments designed to help students interrogate their marginalized standing in the larger culture in terms of their gender, race, or class; and (3) an emphasis on service and social responsibility. These are the defining features of what I call *activist rhetoric instruction,* and they represent important forms of alternative writing and speaking courses that emerged to address the needs of diverse student populations in the United States during the late nineteenth and early twentieth centuries. Such features of rhetorical instruction did not exist in many of the mainstream rhetoric courses at other institutions where white women, African Americans, and members of the working class were excluded from study or, if admitted, did not attend in great numbers.

A crucial portion of this book addresses how concerns about gender, race, and class issues informed the rhetoric curricula designed for specific student constituencies. In light of the present debates surrounding identity and language instruction, writing assignments that take up discussions of gender, race, and class, and the emphasis on service learning, we are reminded that the teaching of writing and speaking has always been a political enterprise. Yet courses in writing and speaking have often been viewed as "neutral" or "apolitical" when they have been conceived as skills-based instruction. I employ the term *rhetoric* or *rhetoric instruction* throughout this book to distinguish skills-based or less overtly political curricula from the activist rhetorics generated by the educators in this study. I define rhetoric broadly to include education in speaking, reading, and writing, and I have chosen the term *rhetoric* over *composition* because of the former's historical association with philosophies of language. Because the educators in this study promoted courses in speaking, reading, and writing that asked students to examine the ideological implications of communication, I chose a term that is more indicative of a sophisticated interrogation of language and the curricular politics that inform the study of speaking, reading, and writing.

As I argue throughout this book, educators in other historical moments recognized the ethical issues that emerge when students are initiated in particular language practices. As a result of this awareness, many rhetoric teachers outside traditional colleges and universities set out to address the curriculum deficiencies of institutions that did not consider how students from different cultural backgrounds in the United States might benefit from alternative forms of rhetorical study. The students of Jordan, Brown, Colby, Norton, and Budenz often faced particular kinds of discrimination in the larger culture and were the victims of forms of intelligence prejudice perpetuated by physicians and scientists who argued that white women, African Americans, and workers were not suited for academic work in colleges and universities.

The Educational Climate in Late-Nineteenth- and Early-Twentieth-Century America

Before I discuss the features of activist rhetoric instruction in more detail, some attention to the U.S. sociopolitical context of the late nineteenth and early twentieth centuries may provide a better overview of the discrimination these groups experienced inside and outside academe. It may underscore the difficulties faced by disenfranchised students to gain admission to and graduate from most American colleges and universities at a time when these same groups of people struggled outside the boundaries of higher education to make strides politically and economically in a world that still belonged to a fairly elite portion of the population.

Prevailing attitudes of discrimination maintained the division between a white, male, economically privileged elite and others who were marginalized in a variety of ways; these attitudes were sustained by a number of widely circulated documents in late-nineteenth- and early-twentieth-century America that I will touch on briefly in this section, documents that presented "scientific" evidence for the inferior minds and dispositions of those who were female, nonwhite, and working-class.[1] Such treatises resulted in the further disenfranchisement of these groups and helped to discourage the admission of white women, African Americans, and working-class people to American colleges and universities.

White Women

Consider first of all that until the middle of the nineteenth century, a variety of social laws severely limited the economic freedom of even fairly privileged white women, which ultimately affected their educational opportunities. Before this time, the property rights of American married women followed the dictates of common law, under which everything a woman owned became her husband's property upon her marriage. Although a series of Married Women's Property Acts were passed in various states to reverse the tradition between 1840 and 1895, the social climate and the attitudes created by these traditional laws hindered this group of women's economic dependence and fostered attitudes about them that ultimately narrowed their options to pursue an education (Foner and Garraty 392).

In addition, the lack of reproductive freedom made it difficult for women to advance educationally. Catherine Hobbs points out that "in 1800 women's life expectancy was only forty-two years. . . . After marriage, a woman in 1800 could expect to have about seven children, excluding miscarriages

3

and stillbirths." Women often quit school at an early age to marry and were soon immersed in child rearing and household chores. Hobbs observes, however, that as education rates began to rise at all levels, women experienced more control over their bodies and their lives as "the fertility rate declined by 23 percent by 1850, and 50 percent by 1900" (19).[2]

By 1890, shortly after Mary Augusta Jordan began her career as a rhetoric professor at Smith College, there were about 56,000 women in attendance at various colleges and universities. This number increased to 85,000 by 1900 (Hobbs 16). Many of these women attended women's colleges that opened their doors in rapid succession in the late nineteenth century. These institutions came to be known as the Seven Sisters Colleges, and they were all founded within twenty-five years of one another: Vassar (1865), Smith and Wellesley (1875), Radcliffe (1879), Mount Holyoke (1888), and Barnard and Bryn Mawr (1889) (Conway 209). While these institutions and others aided women in pursuing their educational goals, the overall climate in the country remained conservative in a time when it would still be many years—until 1920—before women could vote to influence important social policies that played a role in shaping their lives.

In this conservative climate, the issue of higher education for all women remained controversial. Throughout the nineteenth century, a number of documents appeared that helped to intensify the challenges women faced in pursuing a college degree. Edward Clarke, a professor of gynecology at Harvard, wrote one of the most notorious pieces ever used to argue against higher education for women. In *Sex in Education* (1873), Clarke charged that women would experience mental and physical damage if they attempted to obtain a college education. Women who attended college, he said, risked "neuralgia, uterine disease, hysteria, and other derangements of the nervous system," including their fertility, since "the system never does two things well at the same time . . ." (41). Clarke relied on Charles Darwin to suggest that the female constitution was inferior to the male's because of the mothering role in the process of evolution. But the charge of women's physical and intellectual inferiority was not led entirely by men. In 1875, Emily White, professor of physiology at a women's medical college in Philadelphia argued that the purpose of education for young women was primarily to enhance the feminine nature of "tenderness and love . . . and devotional sentiment" (qtd. in Ricks 62). Throughout the late nineteenth century, Clarke's book and White's comments were widely circulated and received endorsement from educators, administrators, and others who believed that grave physical problems would result from women's "unnatural" pursuit of higher education. Unfortunately, there are no statistics available to tell us how many women from a variety of backgrounds were persuaded against seeking a college education as a result of such documents. However, Jordan and other educational feminists often refer to arguments made by Clarke and others in their own defense of higher education for women.[3] This suggests that the argument that women were unsuited to college study was pervasive and exerted considerable influence over the general populace at this time.

African Americans

African Americans, too, faced a bleak existence in post–Civil War America as intense racism severely restricted their opportunities in every part of the United States. Particularly in the South, Jim Crow laws of the 1890s resulted in a devastating period of oppression and abuse. Segregation reigned in the United States as whites denied blacks employment possibilities and voting rights. Lynchings, numbering in the thousands, posed the physical threat of torture and murder to keep blacks in their place, in an attempt to ensure that African Americans would not pursue any goal that threatened the white supremacist power structure (Foner and Garraty 684–86). Yet even in this negative climate, a rising tide of African American protest manifested itself in many progressive changes—in Marcus Garvey's black nationalist movement, in the development of the Harlem literary renaissance, and in the growth of the NAACP (Wolters 17). In light of this progress, many in the African American community demanded a quality of higher education that would allow them to take advantage of new opportunities and become leaders of their communities in significant ways. Nevertheless, the prevalent racism in the United States at this time made it especially difficult for African Americans to rise to these challenges and obtain the education that would help make political change possible.

Unfortunately, government legislation did little to improve the political and educational climate of the time for African Americans. The Morrill Act of 1862, for example, made no provision for Negro colleges. Only three states in the South designated black colleges to receive federal funds. In 1890, Congress passed a second Morrill Act requiring that black colleges receive land-grant moneys. According to Wolters, this legislation had a negative effect on many black institutions because it fashioned "academically oriented black colleges into institutes that fostered vocational training as especially suited to a predetermined, subordinate role for the Negro in American society" (10). In this spirit of "new vocationalism," the reigning white opinion was that only training in simple skills suited Negroes and that they should not be educated out of their environment. Wolters adds that the

Smith-Lever and Smith-Hughes acts of 1914 and 1917 "rounded out the program of vocational and agricultural training and established a county-agent bureaucracy. The county agents then assumed responsibility for seeing that the land-grant colleges, and especially black institutions did not stray from the gospel of vocationalism" (10). In such a prevailing educational climate, many African Americans worked to resist the vocational agenda of the time.[4]

Arguments that African Americans were best suited for vocational education received support from documents that made racist charges about their intellectual inferiority. Those scientists who "proved" African American intellectual inferiority as a result of craniometry (a comparison of the skulls of African Americans with those of whites) increased the educational barriers for blacks in the years following slavery. Many whites publicly denounced higher education for African Americans in attacks similar to this one made by the editor of the *New Orleans Times-Democrat* who wrote in 1904: "The higher education of the Negro unfits him for the work that it is intended that he shall do, and cultivates ambitions that can never be realized" (qtd. in Wolters 5). In a similar vein, Virginia physician Robert Bennett Bean published an article in 1906 expressing African American inferiority through a study comparing the brains of blacks and whites. His writing became the subject of an editorial in *American Medicine* in 1907 that announced that Bean's work explained "the anatomical basis for the complete failure of the Negro schools to impart the higher studies—the brain cannot comprehend them any more than a horse can understand the rule of three" (qtd. in Gould 80). Long after the Civil War whites feared that education would undermine black willingness to work and would create a less deferential, submissive, and dependent race. Thus, intense racism perpetuated poor educational prospects for African Americans throughout the United States in the late nineteenth and early twentieth centuries, and studies by scientists gave academic gatekeepers empirical "proof" to keep racist admission standards in place.

Members of the Working Class

The challenges facing women and African Americans were similar to those American workers endured in the early twentieth century in a nation that was increasingly unsympathetic to the cause of organized labor. In the wake of the 1917 Bolshevik revolution in Russia, a deep fear of communism emerged in the United States, resulting in the historic Red Scare. The Palmer Raids of 1919–20 were one attempt by the government to ensure that a similar revolution did not occur in the United States. Union membership fell from 5 million in 1920 to 3.6 million in 1923. "Yellow-dog contracts" permitted employers to fire or refuse employment to anyone affiliated with a union. No labor legislation was enacted during this period that would have helped organized labor to make any significant gains. Though it was increasingly difficult for workers to engage in social protest, deplorable conditions continued to plague them. Virtually no protection existed for children in the labor market; the census of 1920 suggests that more than a million children between the ages of ten and fifteen were working in industries such as textiles, glass, and street trades. Nor was there legislation in effect at this time to regulate the number of hours men and women worked each day. Work in industry was often hazardous, and overtired workers endangered their health and safety by working long hours in dangerous conditions (Bernstein 119).

Because Americans who worked in industry continued to endure numerous hardships, many labor activists believed that the unions had to take an aggressive stance against the antilabor sentiment that exploded in the United States at this time. They argued that they had to create schools for students that would help them to be more cognizant of these abuses so that they could better resist them. Through the Workers' Education Movement, organized labor invested itself in an overtly politicized curriculum that made social class a central consideration of schooling. In labor colleges and in correspondence courses, this movement built a curriculum that considered fully the literature, history, and language practices of the working class.[5]

Like white women and African Americans, working-class people were no less likely to escape charges by scientists and educational psychologists that they too were mentally unfit to benefit from the colleges and universities of America. Although a number of people studying the new field of the scientific measurement of intelligence argued for the relationship between class and intelligence, no other theorist pursued the argument longer throughout the twentieth century and with as much fervor as Cyril Burt. A theoretical psychologist, Burt made his reputation as a hereditarian in the field of mental testing. He published widely in the first half of the twentieth century. Throughout his career he maintained that there were clear demarcations in intelligence based on class differences:

> Any recent attempt to base our educational policy for the future on the assumption that there are no real differences, or at any rate no important differences, between the average intelligence of the different social classes is not only bound to fail; it is likely to be fraught with disastrous consequences for the welfare of the nation as a whole, and at the same time to result in needless disappointments for the pupils concerned. The facts of

genetic inequality, whether or not they conform to our personal wishes and ideals, are something that we cannot escape. (qtd. in Gould 285)

Work on intelligence by other theorists described the physical features of working-class children and adults and the ways such features corresponded to particular deficiencies in intelligence. Like Burt, many mental testing experts of the early twentieth century such as Charles Spearman and others argued that class differences were in fact based on intelligence differences, and that environmental influences could do little to alter this distinction (Gould 276).

Due to the prevailing "educated" opinion that documents such as those by Clarke, Burt, and others fostered and articulated, women, African Americans, and members of the working class faced tremendous academic challenges. The pedagogical responses of the educators in this study, then, are particularly striking when considered in terms of the times in which they were generated. Clearly Jordan, Brown, Colby, Norton, and Budenz helped their students respond to and resist these prejudices and the forms of oppression they gave rise to in times when the opposition to their academic possibilities was fierce. Significant as well is that students had the opportunity to examine their marginalization in the context of the rhetoric classroom, where the relationship between language and the reality it delineates became a crucial consideration within the curriculum. Although these responses to educational inequalities emerged in another historical moment, they have much to teach us about our own efforts to shape writing and speaking curricula that do not ignore gender, race, and class differences. Moreover, I hope this entire study suggests the important role that educational history can play in discussions that shape rhetoric curricula specifically and educational policy more generally.

Activist Versus Mainstream Rhetoric Instruction

Given the legal and ideological obstacles that white women, African Americans, and members of the working class encountered in the larger culture, it is not surprising that students from these groups were seldom admitted to most traditional colleges and universities of late-nineteenth- and early-twentieth-century America. Though certainly students outside a privileged portion of the population that was largely white, male, and from an elite social class managed to gain admission to "mainstream" colleges and universities and succeed, the difficulties faced by many nontraditional students in post–Civil War America should not be ignored. Certainly such students, if admitted, could not expect to find a curriculum in place designed to meet the needs of every member of the academic community. Instead, students were expected to assimilate, as best they could, into mainstream academic culture. It should not be assumed, however, that what I am calling *mainstream* academic culture could ever be considered to be entirely uniform or monolithic. I use this term to classify institutions that did not consider student diversity in curriculum planning even as I suggest that it is likely that important differences existed in the curricula and the pedagogical orientations of those instructors who taught at more traditional colleges and universities.

Certainly no brief summary can do justice to the variety of rhetoric courses in the late nineteenth and early twentieth centuries in the United States that were designed for a student population that was largely white, male, and from an elite social class. Indeed, I share Robin Varnum's understanding that writing and speaking instruction has always been more varied than initially supposed by historians in the field of rhetoric and composition.[6] Of the early-twentieth-century composition pedagogies, Varnum writes:

> Different individuals promoted different methods and approaches. Progressive teachers contended with those who insisted on standards for correctness. Teachers who valued scientific methods contended with those who upheld humanistic or literary values. Teachers who linked writing to personal growth argued with those who linked it to clear thinking or to academic commercial success. Those who advocated writing about literature argued with those who advocated writing about issues or about personal experience. Those who wanted students to learn to write by writing argued with those who wanted them to study model essays or to memorize rules. (16)

As Varnum's work demonstrates, the varied approaches to rhetorical instruction illustrate the difficulties and dangers of using a term like *mainstream pedagogies*. When I use this term, I refer to those courses of rhetorical study that were *not* overtly politicized in terms of the features that characterize the activist rhetoric curricula designed by Jordan, Brown, Colby, Norton, and Budenz—courses at other institutions in which instructors and students had no pressing needs to understand the politics, ethics, and social organization implicit in language acquisition and linguistic forms. In other words, whatever variations there were in rhetorical study at, for instance, Harvard, the University of Chicago, or any number of established universities, it is likely that they shared a common characterization of African American English vernacular as "incorrect" and were not so likely to defend alternative modes of communication by women or others of a lower socioeconomic standing in the name of cultural pluralism. Furthermore, within more traditional institutions, writing and speaking assignments were less likely to incorporate attention to racism, sexism, and economic exploitation from the perspective of those who experienced it most often, since those students were not, by and large, in attendance at these colleges and universities. Finally, the overt emphasis on social responsibility to specific groups—to white women, African Americans, and working-class people—was not a likely emphasis within the rhetoric curricula at more traditional schools. Though certainly there has been an association between the study of rhetoric and civic participation, historically speaking, the emphasis on service promoted by the educators in this study is significant because it targets specific disenfranchised groups for help by others who are members of the same community.

The failure of more traditional institutions to address and celebrate diversity in their curricula is ironic, however, because the study of rhetoric is deeply rooted in the democratic educational ideals of America, which have often been tied to a celebration of pluralism. America's political legacy suggests that its citizens have long valued dissident voices; the Constitution and the Declaration of Independence are political documents that espouse the interests of a wide variety of Americans and their right to speak from various points of view and locations. We know, however, that despite the virtues of these documents, numerous conflicts and contradictions drive many forms of social inequality in America.[7] Within the realm of education, these conflicts and contradictions permeate our educational history. Our colleges and universities have, at least superficially, claimed to promote democratic educational ideals through the creation of the land-grant institutions established by the Morrill Act, for example, and through other moneys designated for the democratization of higher education in the United States. Unfortunately, however, many academic institutions failed, over time, to offer fair educational opportunities to diverse student populations because most curricula did not take into consideration how issues of difference such as gender, race, and class might need to be addressed in the classroom.

Ideology and Institutional Mission Statements

Rhetoric teachers at Smith, Wilberforce, Brookwood, and other colleges and universities founded to serve disenfranchised students viewed the teaching of writing and speaking as an inherently political project. As a result, their curricula and teaching practices reflect the political agendas defined by their respective institutions—institutions committed to particular social groups within the larger formation of post–Civil War society. Unlike the mission statements of more traditional institutions that made a practice of speaking of democracy in vague or abstract terms, colleges such as Smith, Wilberforce, and Brookwood expressed, in varying degrees, their commitments to specific groups of disenfranchised students.

At Smith College, for example, the following statement of purpose (dated 1887) defined the goals of one of the first women's colleges in America:

> The object of the institution, as stated by the founder, is "The establishment and maintenance of an institution for the higher education of young women, with the design to furnish them means and facilities for education equal to those which are afforded in our colleges for young men." The college is not intended to fit woman for a particular sphere or profession, but to perfect her intellect by the best methods which philosophy and experience suggest, so that she may be better qualified to enjoy and do well her work in life, whatever that work may be. It is a Woman's College, aiming not only to give the broadest and highest intellectual culture, but also to preserve and perfect every characteristic of a complete womanhood. (Official Circular)

This document, oddly enough, explains that Smith College aspires to provide women with an education equal to that acquired of young men but without the goal of training for "a particular sphere or profession." Such a mission statement would have appeared ludicrous in a similar document from Harvard or Yale or any other men's college. Where college men took up higher education for the sake of a career, women at this time could not overtly claim to have the same goal. It is interesting, though, that this mission statement does indicate the potential women have to do valuable work despite the gendered limitations imposed on them by nineteenth-century society. To suggest that the education ought to better qualify a woman "to do well her work in life, whatever that work may be" implies that there are numerous ways that an educated woman might contribute to her community. In many ways this document, like the course of rhetorical study promoted by Jordan, shares the implicit feminism I examine in terms of Jordan's work in chapter 2—a feminism that functions outside the realm of received academic courses of rhetorical study identified by Jordan as "male" and therefore inadequate to meet the needs of her female students.

The mission statement of Wilberforce University was much less overt about its commitment to African American students; however, of the colleges that form the basis of this study, it is most explicit in its alignment with spiritual principles. In 1885, the board of directors published this statement in the *Wilberforce Alumnal:*

> Our aim is to make Christian scholars, not mere book-worms, but workers, *educated workers* with God for man—to effect which we employ not the Classics and Mathematics only, but Science and Philosophy also, the

former for their discriminating, polishing and cultivating influences, the latter for the quickness and exactness which they impart to the cognitive faculty, and the seed thoughts which they never fail to sow in the mind. And yet we hold that the Classics and Mathematics, as Science and Philosophy, can and must be consecrated to human well-being by the teachings, the sentiments and the spirit of Jesus. (23)

Despite the absence of an explicit emphasis on African American politics, there is a strong suggestion of the activism of the institution and its curricula in the statement that proposes that the goal of the institution is to "make Christian scholars, not mere book-worms, but workers, *educated workers* with God for man. . . ."[8] This portion of the mission statement suggests, as do the pedagogical materials of Hallie Quinn Brown I explore in chapter 3, that education without activism is limited in its outcomes, and that an alliance between rhetorical study and service would aid the political goal of social uplift for African Americans.

Similarly, the Brookwood Policy Committee articulated a mission statement that was the clearest of all in its description of the overt political orientation of the institution because the position of labor—as opposed to gender and race—was, in the context of these settings, most clearly a social and political position. It outlined the following principles to guide the school in making decisions in the best interest of the college and its students:

> Brookwood is a workers' educational institution. It regards itself as an integral part of the American and international labor movement. In such a desperate crisis as now confronts the working masses throughout the world, with Fascism everywhere save in Soviet Russia marching ruthlessly onward, it is essential for any institution taking part in the labor struggle to be clear as to its philosophy and purpose. Vagueness in purpose or lack of vigor in action are dangerous. . . .
>
> Brookwood must be closely linked with its graduates in the field. Its educational work should be related as closely as possible to actual struggles of the workers and farmers, employed and unemployed. It cannot always draw a fine line between "educational" and "organizational" work. It cannot purvey "neutral" education in trade union situations, for example, where racketeering, corruption or autocracy are involved. It must "take sides." . . . (Statement of Purpose)

This overt political statement aligns Brookwood's goals with those of the worldwide labor movement. It defines the curricula and the methodology of Brookwood's instructors in terms of a labor education that makes little distinction between theory and practice. Clearly, those who articulated the mission of this institution had an overt political agenda in mind; so much so that the board of directors at Brookwood recognized that the institution was forced indeed to "take sides," and that workers' education could never be neutral education.[9]

Because these academic institutions chose to organize their goals around the interests of their specific student populations, they endorsed curricula that could be promoted in an ideological spirit. As a result of their dedication to students whose gender, race, or class may have prevented them from attending or succeeding in other schools, educators at these sites designed and taught rhetoric courses that took up language conventions, an interrogation of social position, and the role of service as crucial components of rhetorical study. (1) Jordan, Brown, Colby, Norton, and Budenz recognized the relationship between language and identity and thus valued the writing and speaking conventions of their students, however "incorrect" or unauthorized such language conventions might have been considered in other sites. (2) They encouraged students, through specific assignments focusing on topics of sexism, racism, and class exploitation, to examine their marginal standing in the larger culture. (3) They urged their students to use their rhetorical expertise to serve others from their own communities, particularly those without access to any kind of higher education.

Such features distinguish these activist rhetoric courses from those in more traditional institutions, though I do not suggest here that the forms of rhetoric instruction promoted at these sites were the only models adopted by those who taught white women, African Americans, and members of the working class at other locations. Nor do I imply that Jordan, Brown, Colby, Norton, and Budenz broke entirely with approaches to writing and speaking instruction at more traditional colleges and universities. I do, however, offer these examples of rhetoric instruction as some of the alternative rhetoric courses that emerged in the late nineteenth and early twentieth centuries in America for marginalized students. Such "examples" are not models or blueprints. Rather, they are instances of local responses to conditions that are both local and global. They teach us that activist education and, more specifically, activist rhetorical study have a long history in the United States.

The responses of these educators to local and global conditions are significant in terms of three common features that characterize the political nature of their rhetoric curricula: (1) an understanding of language usage that is tied to self and an emphasis on the ways language creates world view and epistemology, (2) an insistence on writing and speaking assignments that relate directly to the lives and experiences of specific groups of disenfranchised students, and (3) an emphasis on the social aspects of rhetorical education that make students aware of their duty to others. These elements of rhetorical study situated language and communication courses in explicitly political terms, offering students the opportunity to turn their attention to the causes of their own disenfranchisement so that they might better intervene in the project of helping other women, African Americans, and members of the working class to improve their own circumstances in society.

Activist Educators

From 1884 to 1921 at Smith College, Mary Augusta Jordan designed and taught courses defined by their attention to the relationship between gender and rhetorical practice. During her thirty-seven–year career at one of the first women's colleges in the United States, Jordan published a rhetoric textbook as well as many essays on rhetorical theory and women's education in the *Atlantic Monthly* and numerous scholarly journals. In these articles Jordan voiced her fear that women's colleges would not rise to a high academic standard and might acquire the reputation of finishing schools; nevertheless, she believed strongly that higher education for women should not be modeled on male precedents. Her rhetoric text, ironically titled *Correct Writing and Speaking,* attacks the paralyzing effect that overemphasis on grammatical correctness could have on writing instruction. In it, Jordan challenges concepts of correctness and investigates the origins of particular language conventions. In the courses she taught she urged her students to write about issues that faced women such as suffrage, the lack of educational opportunities, and economic problems specific to women's marginalized standing in society.

At roughly the same time, Hallie Quinn Brown, one of the first African American elocutionists in the United States, crafted her own activist rhetoric curriculum. The author of *Elocution and Physical Culture* and "First Lessons in Public Speaking," Brown became a professor of elocution at Wilberforce University in 1906. Although she was often forced to negotiate the tension between the Anglo elocutionary tradition and a celebration of African American language and identity, Brown nevertheless emphasized the relationship between the study of rhetoric and the racial uplift of African Americans as she encouraged students to use their rhetorical expertise to participate in the struggle for civil rights.

Finally, at Brookwood Labor College, Josephine Colby, Helen Norton, and Louis Budenz demonstrated a similar commitment to disenfranchised students as they addressed the problems of the American worker in the rhetoric classroom. From 1921 to 1937 the activist curriculum at Brookwood prepared students to serve the labor movement as active organizers and leaders. Colby, Norton, and Budenz taught writing and speaking courses on the Brookwood campus, but they also designed correspondence courses and created materials that could be used by other rhetoric teachers in the workers' education movement. Unlike Jordan and Brown, none of these instructors authored rhetoric texts that were used by Brookwood students or other nontraditional students of rhetoric; consequently, in the case of Brookwood, I explore the pedagogical materials of Colby, Norton, and Budenz to obtain the deep pedagogical and political overview that the textbooks of Jordan and Brown supply. In each case, however, the materials of these educators reflect a political agenda directed to specific student constituencies. Whether in the form of textbooks, classroom assignments, handouts, or educational treatises, the activist principles embedded in these curricula distinguish rhetorical education at these sites from the curricula at more traditional institutions.

Rhetoric and the Activist Curriculum: Pedagogical Constructs

Language Conventions and Identity

Whether the course was elocution, composition, or public speaking, Jordan, Brown, Colby, Norton, and Budenz valued the linguistic differences that characterized communities of white women, African Americans, and members of the working class, and they understood the important relationship between language conventions and identity. Therefore, these educators drew attention to language "deviations" of their students in ways that did not simply divide language practices into "correct" and "incorrect" English. Because they recognized and respected the ways that language is tied to a sense of self and community, these rhetoric teachers explored the nature of different language conventions and their origins even as they emphasized, within their curricula, the relationship between standard English and social rewards.

For example, in her rhetoric text, entitled *Correct Writing and Speaking* (a text that was used in women's clubs), Jordan challenges the very concept of correctness and directs her attention to the process by which language conventions are asserted and maintained. Implicit in her argument are many ideas central to a consideration of gender and learning, particularly Jordan's assertion that some women's lack of formal education might result in a sense of inadequacy and inferiority in certain rhetorical occasions where "correct" rhetorical practice has historically been defined by men. As a result, she argues that "there is no one correct way of writing or of speaking English. Within certain limits, there are many ways of writing and speaking correctly" (36). To prove this point, Jordan invokes an extensive history of the English language in her text that demonstrates how language conventions evolve over time. The result is an argument that resists the rigidity of much nineteenth-century rhetorical theory and allows her to indirectly acknowledge the relationship between language and identity and to create a gendered course of rhetorical study.

Like Jordan, Brown recognized the tension between the language conventions of disenfranchised student populations and the social and economic rewards offered to those who write and speak in the sanctioned modes of a dominant discourse community. As a result, Brown's instructional materials exhibit this tension as they negotiate between various rhetorical traditions. While stressing many standard aspects of traditional elocution theory, Brown also includes within her materials numerous selections written in African American vernacular, pieces that celebrate African American language and identity.

In a similar way, Colby, Norton, and Budenz demonstrated an awareness of diverse language practices and the issues of identity tied to them; thus, they recognized that their students could use working-class vernacular in practical and strategic ways to convince others to join local unions and support the labor movement in general. Insofar as workers' education was concerned, these educators realized that they could not hope to be successful in union recruitment if their students utilized only academic discourse. Because Brookwood students were educated to serve the labor movement, they needed to reach many different audiences, audiences that included union and government officials, as well as other workers. To respond effectively to these rhetorical occasions, students needed an awareness of language that would enable them to choose the mode of communication best suited to a wide variety of situations. Often rhetoric teachers at Brookwood urged students to write and speak in a vernacular that many academic institutions would have considered poor or incorrect English; however, those who attended Brookwood were encouraged to write and speak in a particular manner in order to reach specific audiences that might have found academic discourse less persuasive.

The Politics of Knowledge: Curriculum and Critical Consciousness

Another significant pedagogical feature of the curricula generated by these activist educators speaks to gender, race, and class through the provision of writing and speaking assignments linked to events in the lives of their students. The majority of writing and speaking assignments asked students to explore the nature of their own disenfranchisement, specifically the ways in which sexism, racism, and economic exploitation affected their lives. By offering students particular kinds of assignments designed to help them to critique their own social location, Jordan, Brown, Colby, Norton, and Budenz encouraged students to achieve what is referred to by educators such as Paulo Freire, Stanley Aronowitz, Henry Giroux, and Ira Shor as "critical consciousness." This term suggests an understanding of the social and cultural forces that create oppression and disenfranchisement and the ability to articulate a response to them.

Jordan, for example, asked her students to write and speak on the subject of suffrage and higher education for women, two of the most important and controversial women's issues of the late nineteenth and early twentieth centuries in the United States. Though she often disagreed openly with her students who supported suffrage, she encouraged them to write and speak what was on their minds and to write in ways that would enhance their opportunities to affect social change in a variety of contexts. Likewise, Brown urged African Americans to consider the issue of race as she extended an elocutionary curriculum to their homes and churches. Through her elocution materials and lectures, she brought a form of politicized rhetoric instruction to those who were unlikely to have the opportunity to attend a college or university. In a series of recitation materials celebrating African American history and language, Brown offered African Americans opportunities to consider their cultural heritage and social standing. Colby, Norton, and Budenz required students to examine their work experience and to call for changes in the mills and factories of the United States, and they asked students to envision, in specific ways, how their lives would change as the result of better wages or safer workplaces. Such assignments were crucial to the development of critical consciousness, for the opportunity to imagine such transformations played a role in helping potential labor leaders to craft a vision for the labor movement and attract others to the causes it espoused.

Activist Rhetorics and Social Responsibility

In addition to studying the strategic nature of various language conventions and providing writing and speaking opportunities for students to examine their own marginalization, these rhetoric teachers urged students to use their education, particularly their rhetorical expertise, for the benefit of others. As a result, the form of rhetorical instruction they promoted is defined by a strong sense of social responsibility. The relationship between rhetorical study and civic participation is certainly one that has often been a feature of rhetorical study dating to classical times. However, as Gregory Clark and S. Michael Halloran observe, this relationship has not always endured as a central feature of all rhetoric curricula at all historical moments. In many respects, the emphasis on civic participation described by the pedagogical architects in this study emerged at a time when the emphasis on the individual in nineteenth-century America came to dominate the rhetoric course in American colleges and the social effects of rhetorical study and practice began to lose their emphasis. "The rhetoric course taught in American colleges in the beginning of the nineteenth century," they argue, "was strongly neoclassical, which is to say that it was a rhetoric of general citizenship closely tied to the public discourse practiced in pulpit, bar and senate of the larger society" (6). As the century progressed, however, and the ideology of liberal individualism became influential through the work of Emerson and Thoreau, the individual loomed large "where the public moral consensus had once been" (15). The influence of liberal individualism is absent from the rhetoric curricula advocated by the rhetoric teachers in this study. Instead, woven throughout their pedagogical materials is the reminder to students that their education obliged them to help others who were affected by gender, race, or class prejudice. In this way these activist educators promoted the study of rhetoric as a deeply democratic and socially responsive endeavor. In numerous instances, Jordan, Brown, Colby, Norton, and Budenz stress in their pedagogical materials the social good made possible through the rhetorical expertise of students willing to become advocates for those without the benefits of education.

Many of Jordan's educational treatises, for example, emphasize the duty of educated white women to their less advantaged sisters. Jordan explicitly criticizes educated women who do not live up to the responsibilities that come with the privilege of their schooling. She expresses special concern for young women working in the mills and factories of the United States and urges college-educated women to remember them. Jordan spent a good deal of time and energy speaking and writing on these subjects, expressing her conviction that college-educated women had an important role to play in publicizing numerous social issues such as temperance and educational opportunities for all women.

In a similar fashion, Brown urged African Americans to remember their responsibility to the many poor and illiterate members of their race. In her estimation, education utilized solely for personal financial gain was wasted; thus, she stressed that it was the primary responsibility of educated African Americans to pass the benefit of their education on to others. It was Brown's conviction, as well as that of a number of elocutionists of her time, that the practice of elocutionary principles would deepen one's sense of duty to others through the spiritual transformation resulting from elocutionary practice. Numerous elocutionary theorists emphasized the development of moral stature for those who made a physical commitment to the principles of this form of rhetorical study. Theorists boasted that like prayer, elocutionary practice offered spiritual benefits. Within Brown's curriculum, however, the emphasis takes the form of enlightened social action. Her curricula and educational treatises push this tenet further by suggesting that the practice of elocution would result in a concern for the welfare of other members of the African American community and increase their ability to serve them through rhetorical expertise.

Colby, Norton, and Budenz emphasized social responsibility in their rhetoric courses by stating openly that their goal was not to educate workers out of their social class but to enable Brookwood students to effectively recruit others to strengthen the labor movement. This ideal was part of the founding mission statement of the institution, and it extended to the pedagogical materials of those who taught at Brookwood. In the case of rhetoric courses at Brookwood, even more so than in the pedagogies promoted by Jordan and Brown, the anticapitalist ideology of this institution affected the courses of rhetorical study enacted by these instructors. Rhetorical expertise was viewed, not as a vehicle to economic gain, but as a tool to enable others to understand the importance of labor's problems and as a way to articulate a new vision for workers in America.

The Implications of Pedagogical History for Contemporary Scenes of Cultural Conflict

To better understand the issues we face in the current moment, it is crucial that we study pedagogical history, for the context it offers is important to understanding both the activist rhetorics examined in this study and present efforts to correct deficiencies in a highly prejudicial educational system. But just what does the complex educational history of the United States have to say to those of us who inhabit a different historical moment entirely, where the questions and problems come to us as the result of living in a time altered by new technologies and student demographics? The simple fact is that if we do not have a sense of the ways in which some of our present concerns have been addressed or ignored in the past, the solutions we attempt to generate will suffer as a result of our failure to attend to the educational treatises, curricula, and educational policy generated in other times.

The degree to which conversations about educational inequality are being carried out in the present with little or no consideration of history is particularly troubling when viewed within the context of a debate that is as intense as it is interdisciplinary. The effects of prejudice based on so-called biological intellectual ability generated in late-nineteenth- and early-twentieth-century America are, to some extent, still active today, due to the ways in which educational policy in the United States has been shaped by the legacy of educational treatises such as those described earlier in this chapter. Specifically, arguments for the intellectual inferiority of African Americans have continued to surface in the last two decades. Perhaps those with the greatest implications for writing and speaking instruction are Richard Hernstein's and Charles Murray's *The Bell Curve*, a controversial study that maintains that intelligence is correlative with racial identity, and Thomas Farrell's "IQ and Standard English," which suggests the linguistic inferiority of blacks. The appearance of such arguments reminds us that many of the old barriers still endure and that they must be addressed anew by contemporary educators.

Despite the evidence of enduring intelligence prejudice, the commitment to diversity in higher education has become a national priority. We cannot fail to have noticed recently that the discourse of a number of academic fields is now marked by terms such as "critical pedagogy," "multicultural education," and other phrases that emphasize the political nature of all forms of education. While these emphases mark an important moment in our attention to this issue, educational history does not surface as a crucial consideration, as a way to shape our responses to new pedagogical problems. In *Advocacy in the Classroom: Problems and Possibilities*, edited by Patricia Meyer Spacks, for example, educators from a wide variety of disciplines examine the pedagogical, moral, social, and political challenges of college teaching in an era of renewed debate over the relationship between advocacy and teaching, but no part of the book looks backward to similar debates of the past. New explorations of how knowledge is produced and valued in disciplines such as history, science, and religious studies (to name a few of the fields addressed in this volume) give some indication of the far-reaching attention devoted to the politics of knowledge in recent times. Certainly language instruction continues to inspire some of the fiercest discussion of all because it is through language that knowledge is expressed and it is in the medium of language that the politics of expression are most evident. We need only examine the recent coverage given to the Ebonics movement and the intensity of the arguments on both sides of the issue to understand why language generally, and writing and speaking instruction more specifically, has become one of the most politically charged topics concerning education in the United States. Questions about the relationship between language and identity, language practices and epistemology, and language conventions and economic gain are among those considerations that make this such a fiercely contested aspect of the American school curriculum.

It would be naive, however, to assume that these debates have no history. As Lawrence Cremin, Joseph Kett, James Berlin, Anne Ruggles Gere, and other educational historians point out, current controversies over ideology and writing and speaking instruction are deeply rooted in the educational history of the United States. Cremin's detailed account of the Progressive Education movement in America demonstrates that numerous educational projects existed between 1876 and 1957 that sought to make schooling more available to those who had been denied educational opportunities due to their gender, race, or class. And for those people who could not obtain an education through more traditional modes, there were study groups, correspondence courses, and lyceums that sought to make self-improvement possible, as Joseph Kett points out in his history of the adult education movement in the United States and Anne Ruggles Gere observes in her examination of literacy and cultural work in U.S. women's clubs.[10] Many courses of study provided to historically marginalized students existed outside the mainstream academy, however, because diverse student populations could not flourish in most colleges and universities in the late nineteenth and early twentieth centuries in America.

Although many educators and politicians during this period in America recognized a need to increase opportunities for higher education to disenfranchised students, little was done to address the lack of diversity in colleges and universities in the nation. Certainly the Morrill Act (1862) established land-grant colleges and was one early attempt to offer a college education to a diverse American citizenry. However, as Kett observes, most of the land-grant institutions simply furthered the elitist curricula of other established colleges. University presidents in the late nineteenth century argued that serving a wide variety of people under different conditions was incompatible with the goals of higher education, and as a result the law failed to democratize higher education in the ways that it suggested it would (226).

James Berlin takes a similar view of progressive education's influence on higher education between 1920 and 1940. Berlin argues that despite the intentions of many progressive educators to change the nature of mainstream higher education, many academic institutions failed the very students they sought to serve:

Progressive education was an extension of political progressivism, the optimistic faith in the possibility that all institutions could be reshaped to better serve society, making it healthier, more prosperous, and happier. The proponents of this effort aspired to disinterestedness, although they ultimately served middle-class concerns. (*Rhetoric and Reality* 58–59)

Berlin insists that the failure to educate students who had historically found it difficult to enter U.S. colleges and universities was due, in part, to the application of scientific principles to educational methods; for the findings of psychologists and sociologists were applied to school curricula and the case was made for the "universal" learning patterns of human beings. By ignoring the important role of culture and its effects on student responses to educational practice, many institutions failed disenfranchised students because they insisted on models that qualified the position of the noted educational psychologist of the period, Edward Thorndike, that "universal" features of human behavior could be used to design "universal" educational methods. Equally harmful contradictions exist in Thorndike's work, which suggests the relationship between universal learning patterns and educational policies, and the attitudes of college and university presidents of this period who seemed to recognize the cultural attention to difference that would be necessary to educate diverse student populations. Both modes of thought, though contradictory, worked against helping those students whom the Morrill Grant was supposed to serve. By suggesting that many academic institutions could not provide an education to diverse groups of students, or that there was no need to vary educational methodology for them, educators and administrators failed to create American colleges and universities that recognized the contexts, situations, and politics of gender, race, and class and their potential influence on learning.

Since little or no acknowledgment of difference existed within the curricula of most traditional colleges and universities, most forms of rhetorical instruction addressing specific student populations emerged in separatist institutions. At these sites, educators, who often belonged to disenfranchised groups themselves, reconceived curricula to better serve specific student constituencies. Despite the differences between the historical context of the past and the present moment, the activist rhetorics in this study can teach us how students might benefit from curricula that address gender, race, and class and their relationship to writing and speaking practices. As contemporary educators everywhere continue to struggle to educate student populations that are increasingly diverse, recovering the pedagogical artifacts of other teachers committed to historically marginalized students is a worthwhile and necessary endeavor. Policy makers, educators, and parents do much to undermine their current efforts to address many of the nation's present concerns about ideology and education if they are not familiar with the specific ways gender, race, and class have been addressed by college rhetoric teachers in the past.

While Americans have long valued the skilled writer and speaker and placed a high priority on instruction designed to yield expertise in writing and speaking, they have not understood the implicit problems in recommending a uniform curriculum or pedagogical approach for all students. Only in the 1960s as the policies of open admissions sought to bring new student populations in vast numbers to U.S. colleges and universities did the issue emerge full force in a national debate over standard English. This historic moment in U.S. educational history represents one of the important events that helped to make particular pedagogical injustices more apparent to educators and educational policy makers. However, more attention to the history of such debates is required if we wish to understand how issues of difference have informed rhetoric curricula of the past and how we may learn from them as we chart a pedagogical course for the future.

This pedagogical history is an account of five rhetoric teachers and their work to promote writing and speaking instruction attentive to the politics of difference. While this history demonstrates the activist nature of particular rhetoric courses, it also describes what happened to those institutions and their curricula when teachers made narrow assumptions about white female, African American, and working-class students whom they served. For in no way could these student groups be considered monolithic, despite the efforts of educators, at times, to consider them so. To the contrary, what the pedagogical artifacts, student papers, and letters reveal are student communities fragmented over issues of religion, political stance, and economic ideology. Though educators at these sites tried to offer approaches to the study of language that emphasized the cultural particularities of gender, race, and class, none of these instructors could focus on any one of these issues in complete isolation from the others. In Jordan's pedagogical materials, for example, an emphasis on gender included issues of social class and led her to remind her students of other women without class privilege and the responsibility educated women had to them. Brown's work, though focused primarily on racial issues, could not avoid a consideration of the ways that issues of class intersected with the plight of African Americans in turn-of-the-century America. Likewise, while Colby, Norton, and Budenz emphasized class issues in their rhetoric courses, they could not avoid an examination of how race and gender influenced their project, particularly since there were a number of African Americans and women in attendance at Brookwood.

These intersections of race and gender with class demonstrate the sometimes submerged sense of the social origin of these distinctions. Class, as I have suggested, is most clearly a social category and the intersections of race, gender, and class underline for these educators the social nature of gender and race. This is why Burt felt the necessity of underlining the biological nature of class: Those who perpetuated intelligence prejudice in late-nineteenth- and early-twentieth-century America almost always tried to argue for the inherited biological intellectual inferiority of white women, African Americans, and working-class people. What the pedagogies of Jordan, Brown, Colby, Norton, and Budenz did, however, was to challenge the precepts of Burt and others who perpetuated arguments for biological intellectual inferiority by emphasizing, in assignments in their rhetoric courses, the social nature of difference and the ways that particular issues of difference intersect with one another.

Throughout my discussion of these educators, their pedagogies, and their students, I discuss rhetoric instruction for these student constituencies in terms of the work of contemporary theorists who use the term "borderlands" to account for the shifting and often contradictory nature of identity. Borderlands theory evolves from feminist groups that have managed to create complex dialogues among groups of women with varying and often conflicting interests. As the shifting boundaries of difference—of "Otherness"—have become increasingly apparent, conceptions of a pedagogy of difference have emerged that view students and student communities as contradictory and multilayered. In their important work, Gloria Anzaldúa, Henry Giroux, and others illustrate the necessity of moving beyond monolithic notions of "Other" in discussions of difference. Speaking of the ways in which the ideologies of the margin and the center are deeply implicated in one another, Giroux explains that the difficult work of honoring difference calls for

> more than rewriting or recovering the repressed stories and social memories of the Other; it means understanding and rendering visible how Western knowledge is encased in historical and institutional structures that both privilege and exclude particular readings, voices, aesthetics, authority, representations, and forms of sociality. The West and Otherness relate not as polarities or binarisms in postcolonial discourse but in ways which both are complicitous and resistant, victim and accomplice. . . . the Other is not merely the opposite of Western colonialism, nor is the West a homogenous trope of imperialism. (*Border Crossings* 27)

What the sites of my study make clear is that the issues of identity that affect learning cannot be reduced to seemingly unified student interests and educational needs.

Unfortunately, however, one of the risks of complicating the ways in which difference is interrogated and acknowledged in the rhetoric classroom is that such attempts may be construed as reinscribing the "melting pot" theories of education, or what Chandra Mohanty describes as the "harmony in diversity" model. Mohanty fears that if difference is explored simply as benign variation rather than as productive disruption, educators will evade their responsibility to emphasize "categories" of difference as fluid social and historical formations and sites of struggle. Indeed, Mohanty's work suggests the need for a new discourse of critical pedagogy, one that allows for less static categories of difference, one that will acknowledge how multiple, specific, and heterogeneous ways of life come into play within the scheme of an activist curriculum.

Like Mohanty, Anzaldua, Giroux, and other borderlands theorists, Diane Elam argues for a way out of the paralyzing constraints of identity politics. In *Feminism and Deconstruction,* Elam explores how an ethical activism might be generated from an ethics that insists, not on defining difference once and for all, but on a solidarity that seeks justice despite an inability to articulate definitions of "Other" based on a language of exclusion. Elam uses the term *groundless solidarity* to "preserve justice as an unanswerable yet urgently necessary question" (106). She explains that

> Groundless solidarity is the possibility of a community which is not grounded in the truth of a presocial identity. Solidarity forms the basis, although not the foundation, for political action and ethical responsibility. That is to say, groundless solidarity is a stability but not an absolute one; it can be the object of conflict and need not mean consensus. (109)

In situating ethics in relation to issues of identity in this way, Elam does not suggest that judgments are not without cause or without purpose. She means simply that "no transcendental alibi will save us" from forms of identity politics that attempt to define Other in politically and ethically defeating ways.

After exploring the nature of the rhetorical curricula enacted by the educators in this study, I return in the conclusion of *Activist Rhetorics in American Higher Education, 1885–1937,* to examine these provocative histories in relation to contemporary educational debates in composition studies. Specifically, I explore present attention to Ebonics, gendered communication, and the resurgence of workers' education in America as events that possess a significant connection to activist rhetorics of the past. I examine the fury over debates surrounding considerations of gender, race, and class in the composition classroom such as the curriculum controversy at the University of Texas a decade ago. Finally, I take up the subject of service learning as an increasing presence in composition studies and examine it in terms of its historical legacy. I conclude by drawing attention to the challenges posed by activist rhetorics, past and present, using the work of Anzaldúa, Giroux, and Mohanty to illustrate how activist rhetoric curricula function well when they are not constrained by narrow articulations of difference.

This historical examination of activist rhetorics is not intended as a solution to the present controversies; rather, it argues that the prospect of confronting difference in the rhetoric classroom is a more complex endeavor than most educational theorists realize. Because contemporary modes of writing and speaking instruction ought to be better challenged by the politics of gender, race, and class, those who generate curricula and policies uninformed by a history of these debates will provide naive responses to the situation if they do not understand how educators addressed issues of difference in rhetoric courses of the past. My project examines the pedagogical legacy left to us, an activist legacy attentive to the pluralism of linguistic conventions, social positions, and possibilities of community. It is a history woven with the voices of students, teachers, and institutional policy makers—voices that have much to say to us in our present moment as we reimagine the goals of education and the role of rhetoric studies in our society.

Hatfield House Group with Mary Augusta Jordan *(far right),* c. 1888. Photograph by Epler and Arnold. Courtesy of Smith College Archives, Smith College.

Jordan teaching class, 1915. Photograph by Katherine E. McClellan. Courtesy of Smith College Archives, Smith College.

Jordan *(far left)* with five Stoddard House graduates ready for a walking tour in the White Mountains, 1890. Photographer unknown. Courtesy of Smith College Archives, Smith College.

Cover of *Bits and Odds,* Hallie Quinn Brown's reciter manual, c. 1910.
Courtesy of the National Afro-American Museum and Cultural Center.

Hallie Quinn Brown, from a promotional poster
advertising her lecture circuit, 1920. Courtesy of
Central State University Archives.

Hallie Quinn Brown performing "Wild Zingarella, the Gypsy Flower Girl," about 1900. Courtesy of Central State University Archives.

David Saposs (*left, at podium*) teaching a class on the porch of the main building at Brookwood Labor College, 1924. Courtesy of Walter P. Reuther Library, Wayne State University.

Brookwood faculty (*left to right*): Arthur Calhoun, A. J. Muste, Cara Cook, Helen Norton, Josephine Colby, Tom Tippett, and David Saposs, 1928. Courtesy of Walter P. Reuther Library, Wayne State University.

Speech class in session at Brookwood, c. 1935. Courtesy of Walter P. Reuther Library, Wayne State University.

2

GENDER AND RHETORICAL STUDY: THE PEDAGOGICAL LEGACY OF MARY AUGUSTA JORDAN

> Among the many bits of good advice from friends and books, the only one that stayed by me in that moment of being, as I now know, "down and out," was—"Aim at the average, don't fire over their heads"—the unconscious irony of Fate! Not one of those girls looked average, and the heads of most of them seemed to touch the clouds.
> —Mary Augusta Jordan, "Life and the Classroom,
> Thirty-Seven Years of It" (1921)

As concerns about gender and learning become increasingly prevalent, more and more educational historians have begun to investigate the gendered curricula of other times. It should come as no surprise that women who taught in separatist institutions often tailored their pedagogies to women's needs or that their curricula diverged in important ways from those of men's or coeducational institutions. Insofar as the history of writing and speaking instruction is concerned, rhetoric historians have begun to recover the pedagogical artifacts of women who taught writing and speaking in turn-of-the-century American colleges, and increasing evidence suggests that many of them resisted or significantly altered the pedagogies of their white male contemporaries, specifically well-known textbook writers of the time such as John Franklin Genung, Barrett Wendell, and Adams Sherman Hill.

One rhetorician who was quite cognizant of issues surrounding gender and learning and whose name is to be added to the list of other remarkable professors who defined a gendered course of rhetorical study in late-nineteenth- and early-twentieth-century America is Mary Augusta Jordan of Smith College, professor of rhetoric from 1884 to 1921. In her thirty-seven-year career at one of the first women's colleges in the nation, Jordan generated a course of rhetorical study that exhibits a concern for the ways in which gender affects the study of writing and speaking. Jordan (1855–1941) also exerted a pedagogical influence outside Smith College through her book *Correct Writing and Speaking* (1904), a rhetoric text she wrote for those who studied writing and speaking in women's clubs. In addition to this book, Jordan published a wide variety of articles on rhetorical theory and women's education in magazines such as the *Atlantic Monthly*. In these articles, Jordan argued for a separate educational sphere for women, and she continued to do so long after coeducation emerged as a progressive educational ideal.[1]

Many of Jordan's convictions about separatist education for women proved instrumental in her design of a course of rhetorical study that exhibits three of the defining features of activist rhetorics that I trace in pedagogies of other educators throughout this book. First of all, in her rhetoric text, *Correct Writing and Speaking*, Jordan emphasizes the history of the English language and its various transformations over time. Through this emphasis, Jordan constructs an argument enabling her to acknowledge the relationship between language and identity. Second, Jordan's pedagogy links the study of argument to the development of critical consciousness. In a series of rigorous rhetoric courses, Jordan taught her students how to construct and deliver effective arguments on a wide variety of topics central to women's lives in the late nineteenth and early twentieth centuries. Jordan considered the study of argument integral to learning to think critically and conscientiously, asking students to apply what they learned about argument in the assignments she gave them—assignments with a sharp political edge focused on women's concerns. Finally, Jordan emphasizes service in her educational treatises, reminding women within the context of her readings and writing assignments that educated women of all sorts had a responsibility to think about less advantaged women and what could be done to help them. While Jordan was not an advocate of suffrage, she believed that her students had a social duty to less fortunate women and that there were contributions they could make to reform that men could not.

This chapter examines the activist orientation that fueled Jordan's work inside and outside Smith College. It traces the subversive feminism implicit in her rhetoric text *Correct Writing and Speaking*, and it analyzes the political features of her writing and speaking assignments through student letters and notes taken in her classes. It also explores Jordan's conviction—embedded in her educational treatises—that educational opportunity and service go hand in hand. Throughout many of these treatises, Jordan specifies her conviction that educated women ought to take up a particular kind of political work in the service of economically disenfranchised women—and that their education prepared them for this challenge.

These features of the gendered curriculum that Jordan produced inside and outside the college demonstrate the activism that was at the heart of her pedagogy. I identify Jordan's pedagogy as "gendered" because of her own conviction that the white, middle-class women to whom she directed her courses had a separate culture, with specific issues and social responsibilities that grew from that culture. Jordan argued that women should be schooled in a rigorous academic setting apart from men, and she was quite vocal about her opposition to coeducation and her belief that women's colleges should not follow the poor precedents established by men's colleges whose pedagogical methods Jordan vowed not to emulate.

Evidence indicates, however, that Jordan's activist rhetoric curriculum was not always received by her students in the spirit she might have liked. Some of Jordan's students opposed her on particular ideological grounds; they found her views about suffrage and coeducation to be old-fashioned. Nevertheless, Jordan aimed to create rhetoric courses that offered her students rigorous training in argument, and she continued to express her conviction that women needed academic alternatives to those she considered to be poor educational models at many men's colleges.

Mary Jordan: Smith College Rhetoric Professor

Born in Ironton, Ohio, in 1855, Jordan was the daughter of an attorney who later became a solicitor of the treasury under Abraham Lincoln. She lived in Washington, D.C., New York, and New Jersey while she was growing up with her two younger sisters and one younger brother. Her father, Edward Jordan, made the unusual decision to send Mary to Vassar in place of her younger brother when the family's finances permitted the sponsorship of only one child to college (Dimmock 1–2). Graduating from Vassar in 1876, Jordan went on to receive her M.A. from the same institution in 1878. In the three years following, she became a librarian at Vassar and then an instructor of English until 1884, when she was asked to assume a teaching position at Smith College. When President Seelye asked whom he should get to fill a teaching vacancy, he was told by a former Vassar administrator: "Go over to Vassar and get Miss Jordan—She's little, but she's fierce" (Jordan, "The Teaching of English" 11). Administrators at Smith discovered just how fierce Miss Jordan could be as she negotiated the terms of her employment. Jordan was determined to get the salary that she desired so that she could finance the education of her nieces and nephews. She also had to face a common interrogation by President Seelye in the interview about her prospects for marriage and was asked "whether she were engaged to be married or thought that she was likely to become so" (13). Jordan, in fact, chose a remarkable career over marriage (most women who married were forced to resign university teaching posts) and went on to teach and publish numerous articles on rhetorical theory and women's education over the course of her thirty-seven-year career at Smith.[2]

Lecturing throughout New England on rhetorical theory, Jordan worked with preparatory school teachers to redefine writing and speaking curricula in many schools in the region. She directed most of her efforts, however, toward making higher education available to women, giving speeches to raise money for university scholarships, encouraging women outside the formal academy to pursue education in whatever ways they could. Unlike many educational feminists of the time, though, Jordan did not support coeducation because of the hazards she believed it posed to learning.[3] Disheartened by the methods of schooling in men's colleges and coeducational institutions, many of Jordan's articles and essays take up issues of gender and learning that have become so much a part of current educational debates led by Carol Gilligan, Peggy Orenstein, Mary Pipher, and others who describe the educational dangers posed to young women when gender is ignored. Jordan's commitment to such issues helped her to design a rigorous and gendered course of rhetorical study.

Many passages in her text identify features of "pedagogy gone wrong" in the form of writing and speaking instruction disseminated in many traditionally male colleges and universities. In the following passage, written in 1892, for example, Jordan describes the denigration of emotions within a masculine academic tradition and the potentially negative consequences of subjugating emotion to a stoic rationality:

> It is a capital error in the education of women to ignore the part played by their feelings. It is still worse to try to supersede these feelings by what is called good judgment based on logical processes. The logic of feeling is quite as important as the manipulation of syllogisms, and likely to be a good deal more practical. But there is an almost hopeless prejudice against a woman's feelings; they are looked upon as the barrier between her and real success; they are popularly believed to be without rhyme or reason; it is thought to be dangerous to meddle with them, and peculiarly undesirable that a woman should investigate them herself. ("Higher Education" 20)

"The logic of feeling" is a particularly interesting rhetorical choice on Jordan's part due to the ways that reason and emotion have historically been juxtaposed, with reason taking precedence over emotion. Her insistence that feeling has a logic, that it is not without "rhyme or reason," gives some indication of the convictions that allowed her to generate rhetorical theory that varied significantly from that of her white male contemporaries as she worked to write a rhetoric text for women's clubs and to create an ambitious, woman-centered curriculum at Smith College.[4]

In many of her educational treatises, Jordan voiced her fear that women's colleges would not rise to a high academic standard and might, unfortunately, acquire the reputation of mere finishing schools. She felt strongly, however, that higher education for women should not be modeled on male precedents and that women's colleges ought to offer women an alternative course of study. In an essay called "The College for Women" (1892) Jordan writes:

> The college for women must solve the problem of education first hand. To that end, it must cut loose from the traditions of men, not because they are men's nor indeed because they are traditions, but because the best men have no saving faith in them. . . . Why insist upon sharing the wreck of educational dogma? Why insist upon ranking as "advantages" the under-inspiration of our over-examined young men?
> . . . the student's mind is a republic of powers, not a receiving vault. (544)

Gerald Graff has nicely summarized the stultifying effects "overexamination" had on the study of language in men's colleges in the nineteenth century (28–35). Jordan, however, offers more than a critique of this pedagogical system in her work. In addition, she develops an implicit feminism. In many of her statements about women's education, we can see how Jordan, in writing rhetorical theory for female audiences, seeks to "cut loose" from the traditions of men, from well-known white male rhetorical theorists of the period, such as Genung, Hill, and Wendell, who helped to define the academic tradition of rhetoric courses throughout turn-of-the-century America.

Jordan, of course, was not alone in her attempts to design a gendered alternative course of rhetorical study. Contemporary composition scholars are just beginning to learn something of other courses of writing and speaking instruction that resisted or diverged from those generated by male theorists and the overwhelmingly influential theory they disseminated. Karyn Hollis, for example, notes the emphasis on autobiographical writing in rhetoric courses designed by Ellen Kennan at the Bryn Mawr Summer School for Women Workers from 1921 to 1938. And certainly Gertrude Buck's insistence on connecting writing to its social and cultural contexts, as well as her own emphasis on personal writing, paved the way for other feminist rhetoricians to consider how women's writing is shaped by particular rhetorical occasions (Brereton 249). Thus, like many of the women rhetoricians of her time, Jordan envisioned a particular course of rhetorical study that "cut loose from the traditions of men." This vision is evident in her educational treatises, student assignments, and the rhetoric text she authored specifically for women outside the women's college.

Correct Writing and Speaking and "The Women's Home Library Series": Rhetorical Instruction for Women

Jordan's rhetoric textbook, *Correct Writing and Speaking*, appeared in 1904 as part of a series called "The Women's Home Library." The series was edited by Margaret Sangster, a Christian women's leader and editor of *Harper's Bazaar*. That Jordan's book was published in this forum is an indication that it was issued for a popular audience, in all likelihood for members of women's clubs. Other titles published in "The Women's Home Library Series" include *Women's Ways of Earning Money, The Mother's Manual, Beauty Through Hygiene, House and Home,* and *The Courtesies.*

Jordan's text does not easily lend itself to either of the categories of academic or popular rhetorical theory disseminated in turn-of-the-century America. Unlike academic rhetoricians such as Genung, Hill, Wendell, and Scott, who generated textbooks for college and university students, Jordan aims her work at an audience outside the formal academy. But unlike writers of rhetoric texts for popular audiences such as Silus S. Curry and J. W. Shoemaker, Jordan's considerable engagement with philosophy of language issues, such as linguistic evolution and the relationship between language and identity, places her work somewhere between the academic and popular genres of rhetorical theory disseminated in turn-of-the-century America. Jordan includes chapters that address the history of the English language; the relationship between oral and written discourse; and literary criticism. Although there is no indication that this text was used in her rhetoric courses at Smith, it does help to demonstrate her adaptation of rhetorical theory for another audience of women, most likely those who studied rhetoric alone or in the company of other members of women's clubs.[5] Moreover, it suggests the ways in which Jordan's pedagogy was informed by her desire to liberate her audience from a debilitating study of grammar and a faulty conception of static linguistic conventions.

In this text, Jordan stages an indirect feminist critique of received conceptions of the social meanings of language use. She does so by her acknowledgment of alternative language conventions and modes of communication and by the attention she devotes to them. This focus is quite significant when considered in terms of other turn-of-the-century rhetoric texts. Most well-known theorists of the time, such as Genung, Hill, and Wendell, never address the issue of language and identity and the barriers for rhetorical study posed by issues of difference such as race, class, or gender. Jordan, however, chooses to explore the relationship between language and identity extensively in *Correct Writing and Speaking.*

As a white woman in a mostly white male professoriate, Jordan found it difficult both to ignore the effects of gender on the study of writing and speaking and to express them directly. As a result, her text challenges some of the received ideas promoted by her white male contemporaries by means of its method of indirection and its focus on history. Indeed, many of her educational treatises speak in more blatant terms of important issues concerning gender and learning, and these treatises imply a great deal about the more subtle challenges to the pedagogies of her contemporaries that Jordan's rhetoric text exhibits. For within *Correct Writing and Speaking,* it is the attention that Jordan devotes to the history of the English language and the evolution of what she sees as arbitrary standards imposed by cultural forces that makes her text subversively feminist.

Insisting throughout the first chapter of her text that language conventions are negotiated by members of communities, Jordan uses the history of the English language to make this point. Drawing on the work of T. R. Lounsbury, professor of English at Yale during the late nineteenth century, Jordan devotes an entire chapter of her book to the history of many of these conventions as she critiques the paralyzing effects of an obsession with mechanical correctness on students of writing and speaking. In doing so, Jordan demystifies academic discourse for her audience so that readers might study rhetoric with an understanding of the negotiation of language conventions over time. Against the backdrop of the Literacy Crisis of the Harvard Reports of the 1890s, where literacy was conceived of primarily as strict adherence to a narrow notion of mechanical correctness and stylistic conventions, Jordan's examination of "language standards" and their origins is all the more striking.[6] Because Jordan's textbook departs from the route of so many rhetoric texts authored by white men at this time, it offers one example of the alternative pedagogical traditions that emerged during this period as women rhetoricians attempted to democratize the study of rhetoric for new audiences.

Correct Writing and Speaking makes a contribution to feminist writing pedagogies, however, because it is unique in its attempt to demystify standard English. Jordan's intensive consideration of the history of language conventions suggests her attentiveness to the feelings of inadequacy that a lack of formal education no doubt caused some women in the face of rhetorical study. Through a text that explores the changing nature of language conventions and the features of context-based communication, Jordan's text offers an open critique of language rules through the effort to demystify them.

Demystifying the Standard: Jordan's Emphasis on Linguistic History

Jordan examines language conventions and their evolution in a fashion that is really quite remarkable for the time. While she certainly does not deter her audience from adopting certain language conventions in speaking or in writing, Jordan asks nevertheless that they understand that the English language might be better learned without a blind regard for such conventions. The degree to which Jordan emphasizes this idea throughout *Correct Writing and Speaking* is worth noting, for it suggests that she had a particular mission in generating an alternative course of rhetorical study.

A number of the passages from *Correct Writing and Speaking* demonstrate Jordan's desire to help her students achieve an understanding of the changing nature of language. Throughout her book she challenges the notion of language standards and those who enforce them. In the first chapter, titled "The Standard," Jordan investigates the desire for grammatical correctness and the frustration so many individuals experience in their pursuit of this goal:

> There is a general impression that correct English is something that the ordinary, plain person may reasonably hope to secure. It is a well-defined safe territory in which the painstaking need not err. It is believed that correct English is a passport to good society where, on a level plain of expression, the gently bred exercise their minds. To speak like persons of intelligence is the goal that most of us set up as reasonable and desirable. And certainly the aim seems within reach. But a little effort shows us that reaching our goal is about our only evidence that it is within reach. There are so many ways that persons of intelligence have of expressing themselves. Some of these ways have little in common, many of them are contradictory in method, most of them differ in the effect aimed at, or the impression made. (9)

This passage demonstrates that Jordan understood why the desire for rules of usage is prevalent in any culture where the mode of communication determines one's "passport to good society." However, it is the goal of her text to complicate the reader's understanding of the origins of rules, for she wants her to understand the complexity of forces that determine the language conventions of any particular moment.

Consequently, Jordan emphasizes the wealth of choices available to writers and speakers over the narrow limits of correctness so often experienced by students of writing and speaking. She stresses what she believes to be a very wide scope of "correctness" in English language usage:

> There certainly is at present, then, no standard English, either in writing or speaking that is easily and cheaply available. There is no one correct way of writing or of speaking English. Within certain limits there are many ways of attaining correctness. (36)

In light of this sentiment, *Correct Writing and Speaking* is a puzzling title for Jordan's book. Jane Donawerth suggests that Jordan asks women to revise their understanding of "correctness" out of her respect for her female audience, noting that readers of this text were expected to speak "correctly" as if they belonged to a class of educated men even though they had not been provided the same educational opportunities. Jordan's insistence that there is no correct or standard English could be viewed as a liberating gesture to help her readers to communicate more confidently despite their lack of formal education (Donawerth 348). This is but one of the ways that Jordan's text enacts a subversive feminism that critiques the study of rules and their origins, for the theme of her book certainly makes the title an ironic one.

Consider, for example, Jordan's sarcastic and skeptical treatment of those rhetoricians who appear at various historical junctures to standardize grammatical practices: "Once in a while," she writes, "an avowed or disguised pedagogue deplores the variety of dialects and sets forth some scheme for reforming human nature, speech, and spelling at once" (*Correct Writing and Speaking* 18). This task, in Jordan's estimation, is an unrealistic one for anyone and much more of an endeavor than she would ever attempt herself. But Jordan's avoidance of a prescriptive grammar results from more than the ambitious nature of such a task. Rather, she appears to be motivated by her understanding of the relationship between language and identity and the effects of standards on students who attempt to negotiate between communities:

> In despair the student of English decides to adopt a classification that will relieve him from some of his embarrassment. He will use a consistent form of English that shall avoid what Dryden called gross error. . . . But the first effort that he makes to secure consistency brings him into open rebellion against the idioms that he has used all his life and that are as dear to him as his home, his church, and his dead. (9)

In this passage and others throughout her text, Jordan points to the conflicts "standard English" creates for those who stand outside a dominant discourse community they simultaneously long for and fear to enter. She understands the power of home, church, and family and the considerable power these forces wield over language instruction, not just for a certain class of women, but for all those people who are torn between these institutions and the academy in the process of learning to write and speak. In light of her understanding of this conflict, Jordan chooses to deliver a history lesson that might alleviate some of the anxiety students might feel about this process of negotiation.

Jordan invokes the history of the English language, explaining in detail how conventions of communication have come to exert so much influence on a nation of writers and speakers craving direction at various historical moments:

> Most speakers naturally incline to agree with Ben Johnson's morose "All discourses but my own afflict me: they seem harsh, impertinent, and irksome." . . . So the theory of a standard pronunciation is kept for the most part in reserve for use when we wish to silence opposition or to confirm our own judgment in our own behalf. (25)

Jordan draws on the work of T. R. Lounsbury, author of *History of the English Language* (1897, 1894, 1907). A Chaucer scholar, Lounsbury taught rhetoric and literature in the Sheffield Scientific School before accepting a position as professor of English at Yale in 1876. Lounsbury's text provides a detailed overview of language evolution from the Anglo-Saxon period through the Age of Enlightenment, demonstrating how community consensus alters language standards over time.

Making interesting use of Lounsbury's text, Jordan looks to the middle of the eighteenth century when "the craving for a pure and perfect orthoepic guide began to manifest itself in a way that required relief" (*Correct Writing and Speaking* 29). Lounsbury, as she notes, gives extensive treatment to the yearning of the British for a standard of English language usage.[7] Jordan adds to Lounsbury's observation that those outside the linguistic majority always pay a price whenever a standard is set by that majority, and she illustrates that this has been the case in England: "It has always been a trait of English character," she writes, "to disregard any estimates of value except its own and to pass over others in silent indifference" (32).

The issue of linguistic variation and the price paid by those who fail to conform to dominant discourse conventions is a central concern of Jordan's text, particularly the first chapter where she discusses what might be called the linguistic Darwinism enforced by so many rhetoric texts:

> Must we adopt a "great man" theory in English expression, and explain all attainments of the less imposing representatives of the race by the much or

little that they derive from him as he appears at intervals in history? This doctrine has not been without its supporters. The use of the masterpieces of literature and the influence of great orators and actors has been cited in evidence of its validity. . . . (14)

Jordan is quite aware of the process by which certain forms of expression are marginalized, though not extinguished, and the forces of judgment that surround particular modes of communication. Thus, she points to the evolution of particular conventions, through the use of Lounsbury's work, turning her attention to the historic debate over the very worthiness of the "English tongue" when the question of translating the Bible from Latin was first raised. Jordan makes this point, via Lounsbury, quoting Thomas More in Middle English:

> Sir Thomas More . . . held with equal firmness to a belief in the English language and in the use Englishmen might be trusted to make of it. 'For as fer that our tong is called barbarous, is but a fantasye. For so is, as every lerned man knoweth, every straunge language to other. And if they would call it barayn of wordes, there is no doubte but it is plenteous enough to express our mindes in anye thing wherof one man hath used to speke with another. . . . And therfore, if we should say that it wer evil done to translate the scriptures into our tong, because it is vulgar & comen to every englishe man, than had it been as evill done to translate it into greke or latin or to wryte the new testament first into greke or latin or to wryte the olde testament in hebrew, because both these tonges were as verye vulgare as ours.' (21)

In citing rhetoricians from this period, Jordan works to liberate her reader's understanding of static language conventions in three specific ways: (1) She lends a historic dimension to the debate over standards, dating it to the Middle Ages; (2) she illustrates that the English language itself was once considered too vulgar a language for Biblical translation; and (3) by including passages in Middle English, she gives visual representation to former features of the English language, thus illustrating the changing nature of language conventions over time.

In this way, Jordan's "indirect" or subversive feminism enlists Lounsbury's work with its impersonal subject position and its seemingly impersonal tone. Although it is a man's work, that of Lounsbury, that makes her historical project possible, Jordan is to be credited for drawing on Lounsbury's history in her rhetoric text designed for a popular women's audience. History is important to her discussion of standard English, and so she appropriates the very impersonal authority of Lounsbury's work, a scholarly book, in the service of what some might describe as a more general writing and speaking pedagogy for a particular and historically situated audience. None of the major male rhetoricians who wrote rhetoric texts used in mainstream colleges at this time consider the history of the English language as extensively as Jordan does, nor do they use history in the same way. Genung, for example, gives no attention at all to the history of English in his text, *The Practical Elements of Rhetoric* (1886). And Hill calls on history, not to demystify language conventions, but to enforce them. In chapter 2 of *The Principles of Rhetoric* (1895), titled "Violations of Good Use," Hill defines "Barbarisms" as offenses against the good use of language, "words which, though formerly in good use, are now obsolete" (24). He sees the evolution and changing nature of language as an annoying inconvenience—a challenge to those like him, whose job it is to define the appropriate modes of communication. In this respect he stands in opposition to Jordan, who uses history to liberate women from the debilitating rules of grammarians.

The theorist who comes closest to Jordan in drawing on the history of language in a rhetoric text is Wendell, who, like Hill, helped to extend the influence of the Harvard tradition that set a precedent for writing programs and rhetoric texts across the rest of America during the late nineteenth and early twentieth centuries. In his first chapter, called "Elements and Qualities of Style," Wendell acknowledges the living nature of language and the ways that communities define convention:

> Dictionaries and grammars, to be sure may codify what exists at any given moment. Regarded as codes, they are invaluable; but at best they are codes of common law, not legislative enactments. The only sanction behind them is that of practice, of usage. Before we can use language with certainty we must understand that beneath all these codes lies the great fact of common human consent. (16)

Wendell goes on to add that what is important is not that language is transformed over time, but that those who study rhetoric observe the standards of the particular moment so that they might separate what is "correct" from what is "incorrect." Ultimately, however, Wendell avoids any kind of engagement with issues of language and identity and the difficulties that dominant standards of discourse pose for some students who might feel particularly torn between the conventions of communication of two powerful but oppositional communities. The early moments of Wendell's first chapter simply allow him to promote his overarching purpose, which is to emphasize what is "correct," if only for the present moment. While he might have used the context of communities to set up a discussion of the arbitrary nature of standards and the problems they pose for students whose language clashes with that of the academy, he does not. Wendell's position as a white male

professor, as a man who was bred and educated for such a particular profession, did not allow him to feel or recognize language clashes with the
academy or to articulate, however indirectly, subversive alternatives to received standards. In any case, the other four chapters of his text proceed to
take up grammatical issues and prescribe an unproblemized standard for
students of composition.

It is, however, for the sake of challenging the received standard that much
of Jordan's text appears to have been written. Though the final chapter of
Jordan's text is in fact titled, "Bad Grammar," it, like the title of her book,
is curiously misleading. For in this chapter Jordan does not discuss how students of rhetoric might avoid grammatical error; instead she argues against
the misdirected emphasis on grammatical issues by teachers whose "bad
grammar lessons" paralyze young writers' efforts to learn to write. There are
"lessons in 'Composition,'" Jordan writes, "that must be seen to be believed":

> Essays are produced, and the teacher races blindly through the product for
> false concords, prepositions at the end of sentences, and, if a person of pe-
> culiarly fine literary quality, for the word 'reliable' and the split infinitive.
> These various exercises are so little parts of an articulate whole that they may
> be taken in almost any order and any relative quantity. And in the result, if
> some pupil should, by a happy knack of apprehension, win through this
> confusion to a sense of literary quality, to the enterprise of even trying to
> write, the thing is so rare and wonderful that almost inevitably he or she in
> a fine outburst of discovered genius, takes to the literary life. For the rest,
> they will understand nothing but the flattest prose; they will be deaf to
> everything but the crudest meanings; they will be the easy victims of the
> boom, and terribly shy of a pen. (218)

Such a critique of this attention to error was quite uncommon for the time
both in texts used in colleges and universities and those generated for popular
audiences. Jordan's sentiments, then, were unusual in terms of the portrait
they present of the debilitating effects overzealous grammarians have had
on young writers.

If Jordan's words give voice to the teacher's perspective on this issue, the
bitterness women students felt about this kind of pedagogy emerges in the
words of nineteenth-century Radcliffe women who studied with male instructors from the Harvard Annex who were heavily influenced by the pedagogy disseminated by Wendell, an important figure in Harvard writing
instruction. Campbell explains that Radcliffe women experienced English
A, as it was called, in an oppressive climate of grammatical concerns where
"their writing instructors either ignored their ideas and commented on their
writing performance or dismissed their thoughts and observations by la-

beling them 'feminine' and therefore nonacademic" (473). Campbell includes many excerpts from student letters and essays describing in detail the sort of writing advice women students received from their male instructors from 1883 to 1917. Here a student called Mary Lee summarizes her instructor's comments in a form that echoes Jordan's critique of writing instruction where emphasis on grammatical correctness overshadowed all other modes of teaching writing:

> There were too many short sentences, the transitions were a little too obviously thought out, there was repetition of thought, *above all there was too personal [an] element* [Campbell's italics]. I must write it over and make it flat, insipid, take out all individuality, and I can do this. For English A has taught me this one thing; to eliminate interest and to write bad ideas in good grammar, as the section man likes it written. (qtd. in Campbell 479)

Campbell's reading of the Radcliffe women's critiques of their male instructors, in this and other excerpts, suggests that these students yearned for a course of study of the sort that Jordan advocated, one that "cut loose from the traditions of men," whose scope of rigid correctness made for a suffocating study of language and expression.

In light of the overwhelmingly conservative pedagogical climate described by Radcliffe women who encountered male professors teaching in the spirit of Wendell and his contemporaries, Jordan's use of history to demystify standard English seems that much more remarkable. Certainly, her devotion of an entire chapter, the first chapter in fact, of her book to the issue of standards and the history of language conventions is quite significant in terms of the ways it diverges from the work of other prominent rhetorical theorists of her time who, it appears, were not motivated by an awareness of the relationship between issues of difference and learning enough to consider linguistic history in their work.

Despite the differences, however, between *Correct Writing and Speaking* and the rhetoric texts of her contemporaries, Jordan in no way suggests that she believed women possessed another language entirely or that she denounced the purpose served by the knowledge of a wide variety of language conventions. Her position as a white woman with educational privilege, though, made it impossible for her to ignore linguistic history and the evolution of language conventions that her white male contemporaries conveniently avoided, and, perhaps, could not even recognize. This feature of Jordan's pedagogy seems important, then, for comprehending the ways in which pedagogies for marginalized students may have been developed in other historical moments: that they arise through insights born of experience. Jordan's emphasis on the history of language conventions suggests, albeit indirectly, that women might have ways of communicating that were rewarded less frequently in the larger culture. She, much more than any of the male theorists who wrote rhetorical theory for academic audiences at the turn of the century, had an investment in making her students understand the nature of language conventions and their evolution over time. Jordan's attention to history enacts a subversive feminism, then, that offers women an alternative course of study in an otherwise conservative pedagogical climate.

Rhetoric and Critical Consciousness: The Curriculum at Smith College

While Jordan wrote a sophisticated rhetoric textbook for a women's club audience, there is, as I have noted, no indication that this text was used in her rhetoric courses at Smith. Instead, Jordan's students, as college circulars, student themes, and notebooks demonstrate, read a wide variety of texts commonly used in many traditional colleges and universities. While Smith students in Jordan's rhetoric courses read and wrote about classical texts by Plato, Aristotle, and Cicero, it was Richard Whately's *Elements of Rhetoric* (1846) that was the staple text for many of her courses, particularly those on argument. Jordan's high estimation of Whately's work surfaces in the notes of student Janet Wallace who attributes the following quote in her course notebook to her teacher: "Most text book makers," according to Jordan, "are men of mediocre ability. Whately was a great man" (Wallace).

Wallace's lecture notes (1889) clearly illustrate that Whately's philosophy informed Jordan's classes on argument. Her notes (numbering some fifty pages) are a fairly straightforward outline of *The Elements of Rhetoric*. Wallace summarizes Whately's history of rhetoric, with a heavy emphasis on Aristotle and other classical rhetoricians. Then her notes turn to an extensive examination of how to design a variety of arguments for a number of rhetorical occasions based on Whately's model. The outline takes up the following topics in reference to Whately's text: those arguments suited to conviction—cause to effect; arguments from sign, example, and testimony. Other primary considerations are burden of proof and the function and effects of refutation.

While Jordan's course in argument demonstrates a clear reliance on Whately's ideas, it should not be assumed that Jordan's use of white male–authored rhetoric texts (the same texts that were used in most colleges and universities across the nation) resulted in a course of rhetorical study identical to those in men's and coeducational institutions of the time. Her teaching of Whately in a class comprised entirely of white, middle-class women may indicate a gendered curriculum that is not obvious at first glance. Jordan's use of this particular rhetorician is cast in somewhat different terms if we consider Jordan's enlistment of Lounsbury's work to demystify concerns about standard usage in ways that, as argued earlier in the chapter, could have empowered her female audience. It seems likely, given her position on separatist education, that she imagined that her students needed to learn how to make effective arguments and to practice them in the company of women first, where they would feel comfortable speaking out and where they would not be silenced by men. Consider that at Oberlin, for example, women were not permitted to speak openly in the company of men in rhetoric courses and debating societies; and at Radcliffe, male instructors failed to create an environment where women felt that their ideas and opinions were treated with serious regard (Conway 206; Campbell 478–79). Indeed, many women students at these colleges during this era, including Radcliffe student Annie Ware Winsor Allen, class of 1888, had a good deal to say about schooling and silence:

> Men who have taught both men and women say that in general women have too much conscience and too little independence. . . . I think, women, besides really lacking independence, add to their apparent servility by their timid silence. Women students often disagree radically and emphatically with their instructors' statements and opinions, often have independent, sensible notions of their own; but they do not dare to express their dissent or knowing themselves ignorant, they do not feel justified in propounding original theories to men who have spent years in study. They are not the mere recepticles [*sic*] which they seem to be. (qtd. in Ricks 79)

Jordan envisioned the rhetoric classroom as a site where her students might learn to speak with conviction; she believed that the presence of men hindered most women from speaking their minds. This is one reason why Jordan opposed coeducation: In her estimation, women and men could not receive an equal education in classes where they studied side by side. Though Jordan's opinions about coeducation came to be considered increasingly conservative in the Progressive Era, her treatises on education clearly complicate notions about educational feminism in the late nineteenth century.[8] As Ricks observes in her examination of rhetoric courses at women's colleges in the late nineteenth century, the history of women's education in the United States is about "how women sought self-definition and self-recognition, not simply how they tried to answer the question of what it meant to gain equal educational opportunity with men" (61).

Jordan's choice of texts ought to be read in terms of the historical moment, as Joanne Wagner observes, for the selection of "male texts" was not uncommon among professors who taught rhetoric at the Seven Sisters colleges. Wagner explains that despite the fact that popular magazines of the late nineteenth century urged women to utilize feminine mannerisms because of cultural concerns about education and the masculinization of women, rhetoric instructors at the Seven Sisters colleges believed that women should learn what men learned. According to Wagner, the rationale was that once women learned to communicate in the ways that men did, "it would be difficult to convince them to limit their discourse to 'appropriate' subjects and socially sanctioned settings. Thus, what might appear as a conservative use of male-authored materials becomes radicalized in the context of a woman's community" (191).

Gender, Intellectual Conviction, and Argument

Numerous alumnae letters attest to Jordan's efforts to teach students how to trust in their ideas so that they could indeed write and speak with conviction. These solicited letters came from students she taught over the course of thirty-seven years and formed a volume that was presented to Jordan at the time of her retirement from Smith in 1921 ("A Tribute"). Offering specific instances of the rigorous nature of Jordan's courses, the letters include accounts from students who encountered Jordan in a variety of classes such as "The Principles of Formal Rhetoric" and "Exposition in Oratory, Science, Philosophy." They demonstrate that a crucial factor in their development as rhetoricians was Jordan's encouragement of their intellectual independence.

One former student's recollection of Jordan's encouragement of independent thinking in her courses illustrates that Jordan saw it as her duty to teach her students how to turn their opinions into well-developed arguments derived from the Whately model. It was up to students, as Marion Sinclair Walker recalls, to exercise the power of what Jordan called "vigorous choice" in their work:

> Sometimes a student accustomed to the highly formalized "watertight compartment" type of teaching would say in bewilderment, "If Miss Jordan would only give us definite questions to answer or pages to study, I could do it, but I don't know what she wants!" That, however, was not Miss Jordan's method. Like our later teacher, Life, she presented infinite possibilities then stood aside, leaving us free to choose. . . . if we gained in any measure the power of "vigorous choice," it was because Miss Jordan did not make our decisions for us, but had the wisdom and the faith, having placed the best before us, to stand aside and let us think and choose for ourselves.

Many of the student letters allude to this aspect of her pedagogy, and judging from her work on argument, it is easy to see why this was such an important element of Jordan's method. She knew she would send her students out of the college to other regions where they required the conviction and skill to speak their minds through powerful arguments. Jordan knew, also, that students could not make powerful arguments if they could not trust their own instincts; therefore, one of her goals was to help those individuals in her courses to take a strong position on any issue they wished to argue.

Another student, Jane Watters Tildsley, recalls the form and substance of her experience in Jordan's classroom. She explains that her encounters with the texts and with this professor led her to cover a great deal of territory, but always in a manner that encouraged intellectual independence:

> Our study of Dryden's plays or Pope's "Essay on Man" led us back to Beowulf and forward to Ernest Poole, and it was for the gay young sophomore to trace the infinite chains of thought which had tied authors together throughout the ages. To prepare for these recitations we had to read voluminously, and then, out of the chaos of our impressions evolve some unity of thought and a definite idea to present to the class. We talked of many things that year, of religion and philosophy, of education and government, as well as the style of Dryden and Pope's idiosyncrasies. And all the time we were being stimulated and inspired to feel that we were not passive receptacles for information, but that we had active working minds.

Recall for a moment Jordan's own words from her essay, "The College for Women," in which she emphasizes that "the student's mind is a republic of powers, not a receiving vault." Her insistence on this metaphor emerges in Walker's and Tildsley's recollection of her pedagogy and calls to mind Paulo Freire's essay, "The Banking Concept of Education" in which Freire criticizes pedagogical methods that regard students simply as vessels to be filled with knowledge (*Pedagogy*). This form of education, Freire argues, does not teach students to examine the world from a critical perspective, nor does it help them to take responsibility for their education. As these letters demonstrate, Jordan in no way considered the minds of her students to be "passive receptacles" for what she had to teach them. Instead, she saw the education of her students as a process of negotiation between what they brought to the classes and what she helped them to do with their ideas and convictions.

Although Jordan was an activist educator, however, her activism is not easily understood or easily categorized in terms of its reception by students. Just as teachers are products of a myriad of heteroglossic forces, so too, are the students whose responses shape the pedagogy teachers extend to them. In Jordan's rhetoric class, even those assignments that could be described as "feminist" were not always received as an opportunity for liberatory reflection by her students. For example, this letter by one of Jordan's students, Josephine Wilkins, conveys her apathy for a radical writing assignment by nineteenth-century standards—the topic of higher education for women. Wilkins writes in a letter to her sister:

> Miss Jordan gives worse and worse Rhetoric Lessons. For the next, we are to write a letter to a woman older than oneself, who is very much disturbed because one is undergoing the higher education. To reassure her, and if possible change her views, and make her in sympathy. The letter is to be two sheets long. I think it will be perfectly dreadful, especially as nobody made any objections to my going to college.

This piece of correspondence illustrates that Jordan could not assume that all her students saw the importance of confronting the resistance women from a variety of backgrounds faced in terms of educational opportunities in the late nineteenth century. In this student's life, the assignment was not relevant in the ways that Jordan might have hoped it would be. It demonstrates, however, that Jordan asked her students to examine their class privilege in relation to the obstacles faced by the majority of women in late-nineteenth-century America. Wilkins, as this letter indicates, could not imagine family opposition to her college aspirations; Jordan wished her students to remember that the educational opportunities they took for granted were still only available to a select group of women in the late nineteenth century. That Jordan issued such an assignment offers a glimpse of her gendered curriculum and the tensions and contradictions that emerged in the context of the pedagogy she generated. It demonstrates the competing forms of activism that engaged women of the late nineteenth century and the ways in which particular issues may have played out in the classroom.

It is clear that three of the most significant subjects debated during Jordan's career at Smith were higher education for women, suffrage, and coeducation. In the late nineteenth century there were heated debates over whether women could obtain a college education without endangering their physical health. The opinion, promoted by Dr. Edward Clarke, that women risked fatigue, infertility, and other forms of illness by seeking a college degree received a good deal of attention in the nineteenth century. Clarke's opinions were echoed by Silas Weir Mitchell who told Radcliffe women in 1895: "If . . . the college life in any way, body or mind, unfits women to be good wives and mothers there had better be none of it" (qtd. in Ricks 66).[9]

Even among supporters of higher education for women there was division over coeducation. Many progressive educators wished to see women admitted to men's institutions, while others, like Jordan, believed it was best to preserve a division of educational spheres. While there is no indication that Jordan's students wrote on the topic of coeducation, that Jordan herself published a number of articles opposing coeducation makes it seem likely that it was the subject of discussion in her courses.

The question of women and the vote was at least as controversial as any other issue debated within women's academic institutions during the late nineteenth and early twentieth centuries. Kathryn Conway points out that the Seven Sisters colleges (Bryn Mawr, Vassar, Wellesley, Mount Holyoke, Barnard, Radcliffe, and Smith) were not always ideologically aligned on this issue. Vassar had a progressive attitude toward suffrage, and students there founded debating societies where they learned to argue all sides of the suffrage question. Gertrude Buck, professor of English at Vassar, co-authored *A Handbook on Argumentation and Debating* with Kristine Mann in 1906, a textbook that offered instruction on debate and provided special attention to the topic of women and the vote (Conway 216). Likewise, rhetoric teachers at Mount Holyoke, Wellesley, and Barnard made suffrage the most popular consideration in the rhetoric curriculum. At Radcliffe, however, the administration and many of the faculty opposed suffrage. Of all the Seven Sisters colleges, Radcliffe was the only one to have an organized antisuffrage club (Solomon 237). The English department was comprised of an all-male faculty from Harvard, including Barrett Wendell and Adams Sherman Hill who are now notorious for their harsh treatment of Radcliffe women in the rhetoric classroom. It appears that the approach to suffrage and other controversial topics in the rhetoric classroom, then, was largely determined by the professor.

Unlike many other rhetoric professors at the Seven Sisters colleges, Jordan supported neither suffrage nor coeducation. She spoke at rallies and wrote an antisuffrage pamphlet titled "Noblesse Oblige" that was published by the Massachusetts Association Opposed to the Further Extension of Suffrage to Women. Jordan's own activism, however, should not be dismissed because it may have been viewed as conservative for the time. In many ways, her approach to a wide variety of women's issues resonated with other women activists who believed that women could aid social reform in ways other than an overt participation in government.

Many of Jordan's educational treatises and antisuffrage pamphlets reveal competing discourses that exemplify the ways in which the enactment of an activist rhetoric curriculum proved to be a complicated enterprise at Smith. Jordan appears to have subscribed to the "separate spheres" ideology that characterized the nineteenth century (Gordon 1). This form of nineteenth-century feminism differs greatly from twentieth-century responses to women's concerns by virtue of its insistence on separate spheres for women and men. While such sharp cultural restrictions might appear to have impeded feminist goals, Gillian Brown, for example, notes the ways in which what she calls domestic individualism provided nineteenth-century women with a particular kind of strength and position from which to act, giving the separate women's sphere an "entitling function," a claim of proprietorship and invention in the development of individualism and the development of self (1–2). Brown's perspective helps to explain how Jordan could have championed educational opportunities for women even as she opposed suffrage. Indeed, Jordan's educational treatises on separatist education as well as her antisuffrage writing are consistent in terms of the ways they reinforce nineteenth-century ideals of separate spheres based on gender.

While Jordan herself often disagreed with her students on the subject of women's suffrage and coeducation, she did not discourage them from writing about a government in which they could not participate or from examining other social and political goals that varied from her own agenda. As the alumnae letters and essays demonstrate, government issues formed the topics of discussion in Jordan's courses and created the basis for written assignments for many of her students. Among the student essays that survive is one by Mary Clark who argues, in 1892, why the presidential term should be lengthened. The opportunity to discuss political issues must have been valuable to the women who studied rhetoric with Jordan, many of whom later became visible leaders in the struggle to obtain the vote and who later held other important political offices. Jordan's former students include Mildred Scott Olmstead, an influential feminist, and Katherine Graham Howard, who later became secretary of the National Committee of the Republican Party (Conway 217, 218). Jordan wanted her students to take unpopular positions, knowing it was important to teach them to use their rhetorical training to craft arguments that would stand strong in opposition to any opinion, even her own. Perhaps Jordan's greatest contribution to a feminist pedagogy in the rhetoric classroom is exhibited in the manner in which she encouraged her students to trust their own convictions in a time when the society in which they lived discouraged it in overt and discreet ways.

Jordan's pedagogical orientation regarding the study of writing and speaking and the development of critical consciousness may also be examined through her own comments about the relationship between the study of rhetoric and the development of a moral conscience. Her educational treatises provide a way to speculate about this feature of the politicized rhetoric courses Jordan taught at Smith. Many of her publications suggest that

Jordan saw an important connection between the study of rhetoric and the ability to think critically. For example, Jordan argued against the popular assertion that higher education threatened the innate moral sensibilities of women. Dismissing such beliefs as cultural myths, Jordan challenged the often repeated notion that women have "embodied consciences" that may be threatened by the experience of higher education. Of this opinion Jordan writes

> We have always been taught that they were embodied consciences, with a moral sense so vital that it is the last good thing to die in their characters, and the first to revive. Much of this is the most misleading truism, women are responsible much as dogs have thumbs, and many of the existing methods of education leave this rudimentary sense as they find it. ("Higher Education" 12–13)

Arguing that a discerning conscience is not innate, Jordan emphasizes that it must be developed through the teaching of critical thinking. Implicit in her logic here is the premise that the study of rhetoric has a particular role to play in the development of such a conscience. Jordan denies any contention that such a conscience is or could ever be intrinsic in any woman— that such a valuable asset could be gained without academic training. Attacking a cultural ideology that exalts women's "natural" moral superiority, Jordan disrupts the logic proposed by some that the ability to think critically about ethical issues could ever be construed as natural:

> This style of argument ought never to have existed for a moment or certainly for no longer than it would have required to point out the unfairness of holding any human institution responsible for disturbing a purely imaginary perfection. The higher education is not called upon to show that it will not interfere with the natural adaptability of women's nature, for such adaptability as we need is not natural. The higher education cannot be compelled to show why it will not interfere with the ideal family life, because the family is not ideal. . . . We do not think of the world as perfect or of life as beyond improvement when we are offered reforms in the name of religion or morality; why do we drift so inevitably into this attitude when the training of women's minds is discussed? ("Higher Education" 1–2)

As a professor of rhetoric, Jordan recognized that the capacity to think critically about moral choices was a skill to be developed, not an innate instinct. Her understanding of a relationship between the study of rhetoric (specifically argument) and the development of a moral or critical consciousness manifested itself in the opportunities she gave to her students to employ what they learned about making arguments by engaging relevant issues in their lives. Thus, while the texts and methods may have been similar in many respects to those of men's colleges, the topics Jordan's students chose were relevant to their lives and the audiences to whom they often addressed themselves were female. Therefore, that this student constituency had the opportunity to study argument from someone like Jordan in an academic community comprised entirely of women must be considered a significant feature of the gendered curriculum she generated at Smith.

Rhetorical Study and the Responsibility of Service

A third feature of the activist curriculum Jordan developed emphasizes a relationship between education and service. Despite her opposition to suffrage, Jordan did believe women had a political role to play in turn-of-the-century America, specifically in service to other women who possessed fewer advantages than they did. In many of her articles, Jordan articulates her belief in the strong connection between education and social responsibility. Most of her students came from well-to-do families, and Jordan feared that the young women she knew would be isolated by their social class and that such isolation would hinder social reform. She often spoke against a genteel class of college-educated women who simply retired to good marriages. Believing that it was the obligation of educated women to help others without economic advantage, Jordan took it as a personal challenge to make sure that women with the benefit of education did not live in smug indifference to the plight of women relegated to an industrial underclass. In "Higher Education," Jordan explains how educated women contribute to the exploitation of women in industry:

> Do the social and economic relations of sewing women and mill girls owe nothing of their hardship to the neutrality of educated women? A hygienic conscience makes it impossible for a college graduate to run a sewing machine more than a given number of hours a day, but this sensitiveness rarely extends to such exercise of the faculty as would stand in the way of buying hand embroidery at starvation prices. . . . (14)

The theme of complicit exploitation of women workers by economically privileged women is a prevalent one in many of Jordan's writings, and its presence suggests that it may have informed her pedagogy in other ways besides those that archival materials indicate. This prevalent theme implies that she saw a connection between the study of rhetoric and the development of critical consciousness. In her assignment to write a letter to an older woman opposing higher education for women, for example, Jordan asked students to examine their class privilege and, as a result, the privilege denied other women without economic means or class status.

The emphasis on service promoted by Jordan in many of her writings in the late nineteenth and early twentieth centuries was not an uncommon one in the work of other well-known educators such as Jane Addams of Hull House and Francis Willard of the Women's Christian Temperance Union, as well as other social activists who were critical of upper-class women whose idleness and isolation led them to ignore the problems of women in poverty. Although Addams supported suffrage and the contributions women could make to American political life through the vote, she was a major proponent of service in twentieth-century America, and she had a special concern for college-educated women who faced difficulties after graduation due to limited opportunities. Addams recognized that a college education often nurtured a social consciousness and a desire to work in a larger sphere outside the home. Unfortunately, for such women, "the family claim" was often expected to take precedence. A college education was made available to women to "fulfill the duties of a daughter in a good family and those belonging to polite society." In the process, however, the college-educated woman often experienced conflict as Addams observes, because she found in herself "an impulse to act her part as a citizen of the world" (Addams 66).

Jordan differed from Addams in that her concerns were more for the student who might not attend college at all and, as a result, might not discover her impulse to act as a citizen. She saw that the transforming process of a college education enabled her students to see the wider world full of duties and problems that awaited their action. While professional opportunities for college-educated women were severely limited in the late nineteenth and early twentieth centuries, Jordan recognized that those women who did not acquire a college education were less likely to examine what their own social duties might be and thus risked losing the chance to make any kind of contribution to social reform whatsoever. It was Jordan's opinion that idle minds made women restless and inactive.

Jordan's educational treatises lamented not the scarcity of opportunities for women to contribute to the social reform of the nation but the lack of educational opportunities for women to develop their sense of social consciousness. Jordan believed that if her students had the desire to aid in the project of social reform that there was little that could stand in their way. There was, in her opinion, a kind of work that only women could do:

> The proposition that every human being has a right to good food, good air, good water, and to get on in the world, needs practical emphasis from

woman. Their indifference stands for the fatal inertia that is the only real obstacle in the way of natural truth. Somebody has said that it takes a whole-souled man to raise the masses to cleaner sties, and in a certain sense, this is all that a man can do, the rest waits for the transforming influence of women on women. ("Higher Education" 15)

In this passage, as in others, Jordan argues for the unique possibilities all women have to challenge social injustices—if they would realize it. As in her treatises that define the necessity of separate educational spheres, Jordan divides the political work into separate realms as well. Just as she suggests that women would not want to imitate a number of the inferior educational methods of men's colleges, so too does she argue that women could surpass men in their manner of addressing social problems. Suggesting that the world waits for their action, Jordan also reminds women that the world waits for them to awaken to their sense of duty. Although she does not say so explicitly, it appears that Jordan recognized the role rhetorical study played in developing a conscious understanding of that duty. For without the opportunity to reflect on these issues and acquire the kind of moral conscience discussed in the previous section, social problems might have gone unnoticed. Jordan's concerns were always to make women of the social class she taught understand their unique privilege at any given moment. For up to the time of her retirement, the vast majority of women in the United States did not attend college, nor did they reap the intellectual benefits of a college education. For this reason, Jordan emphasizes throughout the article, it was their responsibility to interrogate the privilege of their social position.

Gender and the Study of Rhetoric

Jordan's pedagogical legacy inside and outside of Smith College demonstrates that the relationship between women's activism and the study of rhetoric as it existed in late nineteenth and early twentieth century America is indeed a complex one. Her work defies easy categorization when the attempt is made to understand it within the context of her own time. The rhetoric textbook, written by Jordan for a popular women's audience, conveys her concern for students who would never have the opportunity to study rhetoric at any college or university. It subversively empowers women to demystify standard English and to discover their own powers of communication through the careful examination of the changing nature of the English language. Evoking Lounsbury's history, Jordan hopes to free her students to learn conventions even as she teaches them to understand their social nature.

In her work as a professor at Smith College, Jordan was a strong advocate for women's education, in a separatist sense. She feared that women would be overshadowed by men as they attempted to write and speak their minds about a wide variety of issues. Jordan did not advocate a less rigorous curriculum, but rather, one that took up gendered concerns—concerns that have since been addressed by contemporary feminist theorists who have championed separatist education for women on many of the same grounds Jordan supported in her time.

Finally, in her educational treatises, Jordan advocated a rhetoric of service and emphasized the social responsibility of college-educated women to less fortunate women. In this respect it appears that rhetorical study must have played a major role in determining the critical consciousness that she hoped her students would develop in the course of their college education; it was Jordan's great hope that the awareness her students gained from writing and speaking about important social issues would inspire them to realize that they could make a difference in many facets of American life if they chose to do so.

The recovery of Jordan's work and other women rhetoric teachers of the period is crucial to our understanding of the legacy of activist pedagogies generated for diverse groups of women in late-nineteenth- and early-twentieth-century America. We know that a number of educational feminists contributed to the rhetorical tradition in ways that redefined many of the gendered principles promoted by white men of the period; in Jordan's case, her curriculum found its most dramatic enactment of activist rhetorical principles by challenging the idea of static language conventions, assignments on political topics relevant to women's lives, and an emphasis on service. Her pedagogical legacy is but one indication of the ways in which gender informs rhetorical study, and in the present moment when such concerns form the basis of much contemporary research, Jordan's work offers us a way to trace these concerns within the history of rhetorical education in America.

3

ELOCUTION AND AFRICAN AMERICAN CULTURE:
THE PEDAGOGY OF HALLIE QUINN BROWN

> If the Negro Race is to come to real freedom and true spiritual power
> and progress; if he is to enter that larger sphere of life which is not meat
> and drink—there must be a body of God's elect—men and women
> trained to large knowledge, broad vision and spiritual purpose who as
> teachers and moral leaders, shall lift the standard and lead our people
> into a larger life.
> —Hallie Q. Brown, "Not Gifts but Opportunity"

In the parlors, clubs, and churches of late-nineteenth- and early-twentieth-century America, numerous guides to speech making, composition, and letter writing helped popularize rhetorical instruction for audiences outside the formal academy. As a result of these texts, the opportunity for rhetorical study presented itself to a large segment of the population that would not have otherwise received this training. Of the many forms of rhetorical instruction generated for new audiences in turn-of-the-century America, none competed with the popularity of the elocution movement (Johnson, "Popularization" 141). Between 1850 and 1910, public demand for this form of rhetorical instruction increased as its practical merits came to be seen as indispensable in business, community, and private life. As a result of elocutionary study, men, women, and children learned to participate in a wide variety of public-speaking occasions. Though most forms of academic rhetorical instruction had been available only to university men entering distinct fields or professions such as law, politics, or the clergy, in the mid-nineteenth century rhetorical instruction emerged as a useful area of study for the general populace. Numerous elocution texts appeared during this period; targeted at nonacademic audiences, these texts helped to democratize rhetorical instruction in the United States.

It would be naive to assume, however, that all forms of elocutionary training disseminated to audiences outside the formal academy were identical in their approach or ideology. In the African American community in the half century after emancipation there is evidence to indicate that many common elocutionary principles evolved in distinctive ways to serve African American students of elocution. This chapter examines the pedagogical materials and elocutionary theory of African American elocutionist Hallie Quinn Brown (1849–1949) against the backdrop of the work of major proponents of elocutionary theory in late-nineteenth- and early-twentieth-century America. I provide a general overview of the elocution movement to better illustrate the manner in which the elocutionary theory of Brown diverged from that of her white contemporaries, men such as Silus S. Curry, Charles Walter Brown, and J. W. Shoemaker, whose instructional texts were immensely popular at the turn of the century in America.[1]

Professor of elocution at Wilberforce University from 1893 to 1923, Brown produced a number of texts over the course of her career as a teacher and elocutionary practitioner. Three of the seven books authored by Brown speak specifically to matters of elocution and will be discussed throughout this chapter. They are *Bits and Odds: A Choice Selection of Recitations* (about 1910); *Elocution and Physical Culture* (about 1910); and "First Lessons in Public Speaking" (an unpublished manuscript, 1920). In addition to books on elocution and noted African American women, Brown wrote and published a number of speeches and educational treatises that address the struggles of African Americans to gain access to education. Her pedagogical materials confront important issues that educators grapple with today, such as how writing and speaking instruction should address the needs of those who have a linguistic heritage that varies significantly from standard American English. She raises questions in her writing about the relationship between schooling and social responsibility, using and transforming mainstream elocution theory to address these issues. Underlying these ends is the larger ideological formation of Brown's pedagogy, which aims at creating an "embodied rhetoric," that is to say, a rhetoric located within, and generated for, the African American community. While other popular elocutionary theorists such as S. S. Curry and J. W. Shoemaker (who were white) espoused the body as a central component of elocutionary study, most aspects of their work were in fact *disembodied* insofar as they generally presupposed universal principles and ideals in their pedagogies.

Brown conceives of rhetoric, on the other hand, as fully *embodied* in terms of the particularities of linguistic culture, historical moment, and social responsibility. I employ the term *embody*, both here and in the chapter as a whole, following Donna Haraway. Haraway describes the politics embodied in knowledge—"situated knowledge," she calls it—in which the ideological implications for certain kinds of seemingly "disinterested" knowledge are made articulate. In this chapter I argue that Brown promoted certain features of elocutionary theory that are undeveloped in or notably absent from the work of her white contemporaries. Brown lived in a time when a black woman educator did not have the opportunity of articulating all of the social and political implications of her work for her community—the African American community of turn-of-the-century America. Yet her work embodies pedagogical features that stress the situated nature of the curriculum she promoted to honor the cultural identity of African Americans in the post–Civil War era. The legacy of Brown's work—which includes, I should add, many of the contemporary critics I mention throughout this essay who articulate the goals she strived for—raises questions about how educators will address the issue of language and identity in the future, and how, in a new cultural climate, writing and speaking instruction may be reconceptualized in terms of a politics of difference. Moreover, the rediscovery of the goals and methods of rhetorical instruction for disenfranchised students that Brown pursued provides a model and legacy for our time. As educators search for new ways to serve a multicultural society, historical accounts of implicitly politicized instructional materials such as Brown's are invaluable to the ongoing reassessment of ideology and schooling and may help us to generate rhetorical curricula that will respond to the needs of an increasingly diverse student population.

Hallie Quinn Brown: Background

Born in Pittsburgh, Pennsylvania, in 1849, Brown was one of six children raised in a family deeply committed to black activist causes. During her childhood, her parents' home served as a station for the Underground Railroad; as a result, Brown witnessed the escape from slavery of many people helped to freedom through the efforts of her mother and father who, themselves, were former slaves. Brown's father, Thomas Arthur Brown, was freed from slavery in 1834 and came to Pittsburgh to become a steward and express agent on river boats from Pittsburgh to New Orleans. Her mother, Francis Jane Scroggins Brown, was born in Virginia and later freed by her father, who was an American officer in the war of 1812 (Wesley 14–15).

The African Methodist Episcopal church played a major role in the social and political work of her family; Brown herself was a committed member of this church throughout her life, and her affiliation with it shaped her own activism as an educator and as a champion of black civil rights.

After graduating from Wilberforce in 1873, Brown began her teaching career when she left for Yazoo City, Mississippi, to work in a plantation school. Upon her arrival, she was overwhelmed by the need for others like herself to educate the vast illiterate population of the region. In her unpublished autobiography, "As the Mantle Falls," Brown tells of her arrival in Mississippi: "Surrounding me was desolation," she writes. "Poverty and want glared at me" (qtd. in McFarlin 32). Working long hours in the classroom, she managed to have a new school built to replace the one in disrepair and she convinced the community to lengthen the school year from five to eight months, in her words, an "unheard of concession for that country" (30). Traveling to other plantations, Brown gave speeches in small towns about the importance of education in the African American community. In time, though, her work in and out of the classroom eventually took a toll on her health and she was forced to leave the region to regain her strength.

Returning to Wilberforce, Brown became a member of the Stewart Concert Company. Performing across the country, this group raised funds for buildings and scholarships at Wilberforce. Between 1882 and 1884, Brown achieved some reputation as an elocutionist, and the acclaim she secured for her recitations also resulted in speaking engagements, which gave her the opportunity to address more pressing political matters such as lynching and education. A grueling travel schedule and poor accommodations, due to segregation, made her employment with the Stewart Concert Company less glamorous than it might have been. Brown recalls that "We encountered hail, frost, flood, deep snows, bitter cold winds. . . . we frequently drove for miles in horse-drawn sleighs from town to town, to fill engagements" (43). The group was very successful, however, in raising money for Wilberforce University and providing Brown the exposure she would need to do political work in the years that followed.

When the troupe disbanded in 1884, Brown worked in Dayton, Ohio, for some time, teaching adult students who had migrated North from plantations in Mississippi. This experience was an important one for Brown, because it helped her to articulate the need for adult education for African Americans; indeed, many of her later educational treatises address the relationship between racism and adult illiteracy. Years later, Brown headed South again, this time in an administrative capacity to work with Booker T. Washington, when she served as dean of women at Tuskegee Institute from 1892 to 1893. From 1885 to 1887, Brown administered a night school for adults as a dean of Allen University in Columbia, South Carolina. Her campaign to increase educational opportunities for African Americans extended itself through her affiliation with the National Association of Colored Women.[2] Brown helped to form some of the first clubs for African American women in the nation. She assumed the primary position of leadership in the movement when she served as president of the NACW from 1920 to 1924. During her term as president of this organization Brown obtained funding to make the home of Frederick Douglass in Washington, D.C., a memorial site, and she established numerous scholarships for black women to attend college throughout the nation.

Brown's activism within the NACW places her in the company of other African American activists such as Fannie Barrier Williams, Anna Julia Cooper, Fannie Jackson Coppin, Mary Church Terrell, Francis Harper, and Ida B. Wells, who were active in the NACW and who used this forum to establish schools and scholarships, to conduct antilynching campaigns, and to address the numerous injustices perpetuated against African Americans in turn-of-the-century America.[3] These leaders enlisted the help of club women across the country to help accomplish a wide variety of goals.[4] Williams, Cooper, Coppin, Terrell, Harper, Wells, and Brown have become well known for their public discourse and leadership in the African American community, particularly in the realm of black women's clubs, where their influence helped to shape the racial politics and activism of the late nineteenth and early twentieth centuries in the United States.[5]

Brown discovered a number of vehicles for her activism in addition to her affiliation with the NACW. Teaching and performing provided important opportunities for her political work. Through them, she reached large audiences (both white and black) as she worked to improve the lives of African Americans in the years after the Civil War. Throughout her career, Brown alternated between teaching and traveling, giving lectures and performances that celebrated African American authors and African American history. Appointed as a professor of elocution at Wilberforce University in Wilberforce, Ohio, in 1893, Brown continued to tour occasionally to raise money for the institution. In 1894, she traveled to Europe, lecturing for the British Women's Temperance Association and acting as a representative to the International Congress of Women in 1897, where she gave a command performance for King George and Queen Mary (Fisher 176–78). Returning to teach at Wilberforce in 1906, Brown published additional books and articles on elocutionary practice and other pieces on African American educational inequality. Brown's overt activism informs her elocutionary theory and practice and will be explored as a central consideration of this chapter; for within her work she enacts a significant transformation of particular components of mainstream elocution pedagogy.

Overview of the Elocutionary Movement

Brown's elocutionary theory and practice exhibit an activism that is most visible against the backdrop of the nineteenth-century elocutionary theory of her white contemporaries. While the nineteenth-century elocution movement in America had its roots in Cicero and Quintilian as well as in the work of eighteenth-century theorists such as Thomas Sheridan and John Walker, it saw the emergence of a range of influential elocutionary theorists who wrote popular texts, extending this form of rhetorical instruction to a variety of people who did not have the opportunity to study elocution in a college or university (Johnson, "Popularization" 143).

Whether a student came to elocutionary study in a university setting or through one of the texts generated for "the private learner," he or she would likely encounter a few central tenets that remained consistent across various instructional contexts. One such tenet concerns the relationship among voice, body, mind, and soul. Noted American elocutionary theorists such as S. S. Curry, Alexander Melville Bell, and J. W. Shoemaker developed theories of elocution that grew from the work of Francois Delsarte, whose work is situated very much in the theatrical arts. Delsarte's theory emphasizes that "the voice and the body are one with the mind and the soul" (Johnson, "Popularization" 144). The belief that the mind of the speaker could be inferred from the tones and inflections of the voice, movements of the body, and expressions of the face is a fundamental assumption that was very much at the heart of nineteenth- and early-twentieth-century elocutionary practice. The importance of the body in eighteenth- and nineteenth-century elocutionary theory cannot be overstated; indeed, within most elocutionary texts, the movements and gestures of the body are as important to the communicator's message as the words issued from the speaker's mouth. To illustrate just how the emphasis on the body figured within elocutionary pedagogy in this historical moment and the ways in which it manifested itself in attention to the physical presence of public speakers, I quote from a newspaper review of one of Emerson's performances in the nineteenth century. This review describes how attentive reporters were to the body and how they scrutinized every gesture and movement as well as the spoken word to determine the success of the speaker:

Most observed that the eyes . . . were only occasionally raised from the manuscript and then in such a way that only those at the side of [the] room met his glance. None felt that he had the usual platform manner of the experienced speaker. We read of a "shapeless delivery" without gestures save nervous twitches and angular movements of the hands and arms—"curious to see and even smile at" and a slight rocking of the body. . . . The voice, which James Russell Lowell described to the readers of the *Nation* in 1868 as a rich baritone, struck on Margaret Fuller's ear as full and sweet rather than sonorous, yet flexible and haunted by many modulations. But others thought there was little variation . . . report(ing) a reading without excitement, without energy, scarcely even with emphasis. (qtd. in Johnson, "Popularization" 142)

In this case, the reporter observes the absence of gestures important to a powerful delivery; however, even the attention devoted to the lack of effective body language communicates a great deal about the reign of elocutionary principles in this historical moment. In an age many years before radio, delivery comprised an essential part of the message, and the audience gave its full attention to a wide range of gestures and movements that formed a crucial element of rhetorical performance.

Another fairly consistent tenet of elocutionary theory addresses the relationship between thought and delivery. Most elocution manuals of the period consider this issue extensively. Numerous theorists emphasized that the practice of elocutionary tenets help the body and the mind work together to make effective expression of the message "natural," a synchronous speech event. One of the most contradictory principles of elocutionary theory concerns the somewhat odd notion that through the methodical study of elocution individuals might discover a "natural" mode of communication. Numerous nineteenth-century theorists, including Shoemaker, emphasize in their texts that elocutionary abilities are natural and thus within the grasp of any speaker of language. This tenet of elocutionary theory is ironic in terms of its failure to explain why, if such skills are "natural," they must be practiced. Shoemaker contends that what is natural is the gift of the faculties, the voice, the body. He writes that, "God . . . gives us the plastic material . . . we must develop into mature faculties through the formation of conscious habits" (xii). Even Shoemaker's use of the phrase "plastic material" feels "unnatural," however, since it emphasizes the unfixed nature of the elements of speech. Like Shoemaker, other theorists make similar mention of this idea and like him, do little to clarify what they mean by the use of this term. Yet throughout late-nineteenth- and early-twentieth-century elocution manuals, the emphasis on this aspect of pedagogy—the development of universal natural speech patterns out of amorphous material—is fairly consistent.

Such ideas appear to claim for elocutionary theory the supposition that what is natural for one individual is natural for another. We see how the promotion of universal notions of instruction could spring from such an assumption. But with such great emphasis on the body and its role in effective rhetorical performance, one must wonder how the message or the pedagogy is altered by race, gender, or other embodied differences. What if the body from which the voice is issued is black? What if it is female? What if the language delivered by the speaker is not standard American English? These are questions that most theorists fail to answer directly; generally, they ignore them altogether. Still, mainstream elocutionary theorist Alexander Melville Bell *does* address linguistic diversity and other variances in community-specific communication practices in a fashion that is uncharacteristic of many of his contemporaries. In his introduction to *The Principles of Elocution* (1878), he provides an interesting response to the challenge that varieties of English present to elocutionary study and practice. Of them, Bell writes:

> Elocution has . . . a special application to the language or dialect employed, that the elements and vocables of each may be pronounced according to its own standard of correctness;—that being correct in one, which is incorrect in another. Thus, in the elocution of the northern British, the Irish, the New England and other American dialects of our tongue—for all dialects may have their elocution, or effective utterance—the vowels a and o, and the letter r, have different pronunciations from those which obtain in the southern dialects of England. The student of elocution should be capable of discriminating these and all similar differences. He should not be enslaved to the peculiarities of any dialect; he may when occasion requires, speak English like an Englishman, Scotch like a Scotchman, and Irish like an Irishman; but his reading should not be imbued with the characteristics of Irish or Scotch or of any local pronunciation when he delivers the language of Shakespeare, of Milton, or of Addison. (xviii–xix)

Bell's insistence that "the elements and vocables" of other varieties of English have their "own standard of correctness" may indicate why the field of elocution was attractive to Brown, for while his portrait of the discipline does not address African American vernacular directly, it gives linguistic integrity to many regional and ethnic forms of the language. On the other hand, Bell emphasizes that no speaker should be "enslaved to the peculiarities of any dialect," that he or she should move between varieties of English with relative ease and comfort. Such a claim for the merits of elocutionary study illustrates that some theorists were willing to acknowledge the legitimacy of other varieties of English even as they championed the standard

English present in many of the selections commonly found in reciter texts they edited. As I emphasize in the later portions of this chapter, it is in the reciter texts where the differences between Brown's pedagogy and that of her contemporaries are most apparent. Brown's work diverges sharply from that of others in its presentation of numerous selections in black English vernacular, selections that allow African Americans to speak for themselves about their own experiences in a language that is essential to the articulation of that reality.

Brown's Activist Pedagogy

Brown addressed the educational needs of African Americans in turn-of-the-century America by resisting certain practices of noted mainstream elocutionary pedagogues, leaving her signature on elocutionary theory and curricula in the texts she directed to the African American community. In *Bits and Odds: A Choice Selection of Recitations* (1880), *Elocution and Physical Culture* (about 1910), and "First Lessons in Public Speaking" (an unpublished manuscript—1920), Brown alters traditional elocution pedagogy in three specific ways. First of all, she engenders pride in the language of the black community by including many selections written in African American vernacular English in her reciter text, *Bits and Odds*. While she also includes pieces found in more traditional books of this nature, the presence of selections written in African American vernacular English represents a recognition, absent from other reciter texts, of the relationship between local communities and elocutionary practice. This kind of inclusion suggests that Brown valued her African American linguistic heritage in ways that white elocutionists did not or could not and that she believed it was important to instill linguistic pride in the African American community.

Second, in her reciter text promoting African American history and literature (*Bits and Odds*), Brown successfully launches a critique of racism in America, reclaiming important aspects of African American history marginalized within accounts by white historians of U.S. history such as the horrors of slavery, for example, and the black military presence during the Civil War. Many of the pieces she includes are by black authors such as Frances Harper and George H. Baker, and W. B. Dick, names that never appear in reciter texts edited by white authors. By promoting such a range of African American authors as well as pieces that revise American history in terms of African American literary contributions, Brown positions herself ideologically against white editors of reciter texts who simply erase African Americans from American history in the collections of recitations they published.

Finally, Brown emphasizes social responsibility as a social and communal aim of pedagogy by stressing the changes in character likely to occur in individuals as a result of the practice of elocutionary study. While many other theorists of Brown's era advocate elocution for the attainment of taste and a sharper mind, benefits that could be translated into economic gain, Brown champions elocution for the moral transformation she believed it could bring to individuals and to the community through political action. As a result, she emphasizes heightened social consciousness as a benefit of elocutionary study. All of these aims—the inclusion of African American vernacular English, of African American history, and of social responsibility as "texts" within her pedagogical guides—situate the individual within larger social formations and in so doing recognize linguistic activity as both an individual and social activity.

Bits and Odds: Brown's Celebration of African American Vernacular English

Motivated by what appears to have been a high regard for the African American linguistic tradition and its various manifestations in the literature of African American writers, Brown's reciter text, *Bits and Odds,* diverges significantly from the tradition established by other elocutionary theorists. Under the pretense of education and entertainment, she presents her pieces in ways that celebrate the language and modes of expression specific to the African American community; indeed, Brown includes selections in African American English vernacular on subjects particular to African American experience that are notably absent from the texts of others.

Generally, elocution texts produced in late-nineteenth- and early-twentieth-century America fall into one of three categories: (1) instructional manuals offering instruction in breathing, gesture, pronunciation, and other elocutionary principles; (2) reciter texts comprised of stories, poems, and speeches for practice and performance; and (3) texts combining both instructional materials and selections for oral presentation. Reciter texts, in particular, were popular cultural artifacts of the time. Found in many homes throughout the nation where individuals sought to enhance their rhetorical expertise, these texts anthologized a wide variety of selections that were used for family recitations, a form of entertainment in the home.

Because so many of Brown's selections in *Bits and Odds* are not the canonized "great works" commonly found in the reciter texts edited by other elocutionists, they offer an important challenge to the elitist curriculum generated by so many of the popular elocutionary theorists who were predominantly white and male. Particularly interesting is Brown's inclusion of selections written in black English vernacular, selections not generally anthologized by white elocutionary theorists. While many mainstream elocutionary theorists promoted the idea that good speaking abilities might be obtained through the oral performance of great works, the promotion of such an ideal raises questions about canonized selections generally promoted in a spirit of "good taste." As Johnson observes, "a prominent claim of nineteenth-century rhetorical theory was the assumption that critical study of great masterpieces cultivates taste and an appreciation of rhetorical style" (*Nineteenth-Century Rhetoric* 75–84). But one may ask, as many have in recent challenges to canonized literary works in schools and universities, how are "great masterpieces" determined? Whose linguistic standards and conventions of taste shape the measurements by which works are judged? In sharp contrast to the mainstream elocutionary canon developed by other elocutionary editors, Brown's collection of poems and readings challenge the elitist aspects of such collections by capturing particularities of African American speech. In them, she defines her community-specific elocutionary curriculum and sets herself apart from other editors of similar texts who did not include such selections.

Some might observe a tension, however, between the pedagogical advice Brown offers in her instructional elocution texts regarding punctuation and the actual linguistic manifestations that appear in her collection of recitations. In this excerpt from *Elocution and Physical Culture,* for example, Brown articulates a point of view that was quite common in other elocutionary texts that promoted standard English pronunciations, a view that appears to oppose the use of African American English vernacular:

> Faults in pronunciation early contracted are suffered and gain strength by habit and grow so inveterate by time as to become almost incurable. A mere knowledge of the right way, will not correct the fault. There must be a frequent repetition of the right way until the correct form will root out the wrong way. (19)

The "right way" advocated by Brown in this context appears to be standard English; yet this kind of pedagogical advice in *Elocution and Physical Culture* is often contradicted by many of the selections Brown includes in *Bits and Odds*, selections that appear to promote another view of pronunciation entirely. The following is an excerpt from "Apples" (author unknown), a piece that Brown characterizes as "An Original Negro Lecture" and one of many selections in *Bits and Odds* written in African American English vernacular.

Well you all know dat de apple tree was the sacred vegetable ob de garden ob Eden till de sly an' insinuating sea-serpent crawled out ob de river on Friday mornen, bit off an apple, made "apple-jack," handed de jug to Eve, she took a sip, den handed it to Adam.—Adam took anoder, by which bofe got topseycated an' fell down de hill ob Paradise, an' in consequence darof, de whole woman race an' human race fell down casmash, like speckled apples from a tree in a stormado. Oh! what a fall war dar, my hearers, when you an' me, an' I, an' all drapt down togedder, an' de sarpent flapped his forked tongue in fatissaction. (92–93)

Most other reciter texts edited by other elocutionists avoid the use of African American vernacular English altogether. Popular reciters such as *The Delsarte Recitation Book* and *The New Century Perfect Speaker* are fairly consistent in their maintenance of a canon of works by Shakespeare, Poe, Tennyson, and other authors who wrote from a linguistic tradition defined by the dominant language conventions of a particular historical moment. However, Brown's selection of works—written in African American vernacular English—is puzzling when compared with the advice she offers concerning standard English pronunciations. This particular passage, for example, illustrates the linguistic collision between the reciter book selections and the pedagogical advisement Brown enacts time and time again throughout her work. In this excerpt, Brown creates the difficult balance between the general and particular through a general Christian story articulated in a particular discourse—a story of the dominant culture that becomes a resource for the black community through the use of African American vernacular English.

While whites stereotyped and denigrated African American vernacular English in such forms as the Uncle Remus tales and minstrel shows, Brown celebrates African American language and culture in the context of her reciter manual for many of the same reasons as does Zora Neale Hurston. Critics often took Hurston to task for her textual use of African American English vernacular and argued that it was degrading to blacks. In fact, quite the opposite was true. Mary Helen Washington observes that in a time when many well-educated blacks sought to remove traces of their background, "when a high-class Negro virtue was not 'to act one's color,' Zora not only celebrated the distinctiveness of black culture, but saw those traditional black folkways as marked improvements over the imaginative wasteland of white society" (Washington 15).[6] As a folklorist and fiction writer, Hurston depicted important aspects of African American English throughout her work. In many respects, Brown became a kind of folklorist as well, for like Hurston, she considers the linguistic heritage of African Americans to be a rich resource worth preserving, a language capable of articulating African American experiences in a way that no other language can.

Brown's inclusion of selections where African Americans speak for themselves in their own language represents a significant departure from the reciter texts disseminated by mainstream elocutionists. For Brown, as for Hurston, the message and the reality articulated in the message could not be separated from the language used to express it. Henry Louis Gates explains that this is a union that has been observed by black writers throughout history:

> What we are privileged to witness here is the (political, semantic) confrontation between two parallel discursive universes: the black American linguistic circle and the white. . . . We bear witness here to a protracted argument over the nature of the sign itself, with the black vernacular discourse proffering its critique of the sign as the difference that blackness makes within the larger political culture and its historical unconscious. (45)

The difference that blackness makes, in other words, is the difference of embodiment, the mark that is both there and not there in a language that is both black and white. By combining community-specific discourse with the standard English pronunciation guides she advocates in her elocution manuals, Brown may have been elevating the tradition without sanctioning it for public performances. Paul Laurence Dunbar, for example, wrote poetry and short stories, both in African American vernacular and in the language of wider usage. This is not an uncommon practice within the history of the African American linguistic tradition, as Gates explains, for the confrontation between African American culture and racism exists historically in the manifestation of inventive linguistic strategies generated in somewhat ambiguous terms for the sake of cultural survival.

African American History in *Bits and Odds*

Brown's celebration of the linguistic heritage of African Americans, however, is not the only evidence of her dissemination of an embodied rhetoric. Deeply committed to African American history, Brown makes it a central feature of her pedagogy, offering African Americans opportunities to recite revised narratives about their cultural location. In this respect, Brown articulates a pedagogy highlighting the ideology of language and history and its implications for elocutionary study. Throughout *Bits and Odds*, Brown showcases African American history, including pieces that depict important historical events such as the Battle of Port Hudson, where black forces helped to defeat the Confederacy, or slave narratives that define the history of black oppression in America. The inclusion of such selections indicate Brown's commitment to keeping this history alive for black and white audiences alike. Perhaps Brown realized, too, that many who might have listened to these selections would never be literate enough to read them; therefore, she may have hoped to pass on African American history to a less privileged audience.

By including this poem by George H. Baker in *Bits and Odds*, Brown ensures that her audience will never forget the important contribution black soldiers made to the Civil War:

THE BLACK REGIMENT: THE BATTLE OF PORT HUDSON, 26 MAY, 1863

Dark as the clouds of even,
Ranked in the western heaven,
Waiting the breath that lifts
All the dead mass, and drifts
Tempest and falling brand
O'er a ruined land;—
So still and orderly,
Arm to arm, knee to knee,
Waiting the great event
Stands the black regiment. . . .
"Now," the flag-sergeant cried,
"Through death and hell betide,
Let the whole nation see
If we are fit to be free
In this land; or bound
Down like the whining hound—
Bound with red stripes of pain
In our cold chains again!"
Oh! what a shout there went
from the black regiment!

(90–91)

Brown presents, in selections such as this one, images of black Americans that are notably absent from other reciter texts that focus on the Revolutionary War, the contributions of the Founding Fathers and other Caucasian political figures, as well as a wide variety of other topics that promote an unreflective nationalism. Brown's reciter text, however, critiques the ideology present in mainstream reciters in numerous selections that offer another version of American experience.

While numerous reciter texts by mainstream elocutionists often include speeches that take up the abolitionist cause, such speeches are invariably in the voice of whites who speak for blacks and do not contain examples of blacks speaking for themselves. While it is notable that many nineteenth-century reciter texts contain selections about the mistreatment of blacks and the horrors of slavery, these selections are not from an African American point of view. Eerily absent from reciter texts such as *The New Century Perfect Speaker, Bell's Standard Elocutionist*, and other popular elocution manuals are the voices of African Americans themselves who speak in their own language about the reality of African American experience in ways that revise or challenge other accounts.

The critique of white supremacist culture through literature or other cultural forms has become a crucial aim of twentieth-century multiculturalism. Cornel West calls attention to the damage done by historical narratives that degrade or ignore minorities, tracing a feeling of invisibility and dislocation to narrow cultural representations. He notes how new narratives help to disrupt those that promote oppression and racial disdain:

> Every modern Black person, especially cultural disseminators, encounters this problematic of invisibility and namelessness. The initial Black Diaspora response was a mode of resistance that was *moralistic in content* and *communal in character* [West's italics]. That is, the fight for representation and recognition highlighted moral judgments regarding Black "positive" images over and against White supremacist stereotypes. These images "re-presented" monolithic and homogeneous Black communities in a way that could displace past misrepresentations of these communities. (27)

West articulates a political goal that Brown embodies in her texts but does not express outright. His description of resistance in the modes of "morality" and "community" precisely describes Brown's pedagogical project, for Brown's inclusion of important African American historical events challenges and resists white-supremacist historical narratives that permeated other parts of American culture in turn-of-the-century America. Her efforts are significant indeed, when considered in the present context. More than one hundred years after the publication of *Bits and Odds*, African American history is still slowly making its way into cultural texts that have long ignored the cultural heritage of African Americans.

While Brown's challenge to historians and their erasure of African American history occurs within the relatively nonthreatening site of the reciter manual, the strategic importance of Brown's dissemination of African American history to African Americans should not be overlooked. For Brown's reciter text addresses the "problematic of invisibility and namelessness" that West describes by allowing African Americans to speak about their experiences in their own voices through the work of African American writers collected in *Bits and Odds*. Consider the last stanzas of "The Dying Bondsman," for example, a poem by black poet and novelist Frances Harper, that tells the story of a slave ("bondsman") on his deathbed who had been an Afric chieftain:

"Master," said the dying chieftain,
"Home and friends I soon shall see;
But before I reach my country,
Master write that I am free;

"For the spirits of my fathers
Would shrink back from me in pride,
If I told them at our greeting
I a slave had lived and died;—

"Give me the precious token,
That my kindred dead may see—
Master! write it, write it quickly!
Master! write that I am free!"

At his earnest plea the master
Wrote for him the glad release,
O'er his wan and wasted features
Flitted one sweet smile of peace.

Eagerly he grasped the writing;
"I am free!" at last he said.
Backward fell upon the pillow,
He was free among the dead.

(33–34)

Although Harper's poem is not written in African American vernacular English, it represents the kind of historical narrative that disrupts an unproblemized nationalism that erases the history of other particular members of a diverse citizenry. The very sentimentality of verse and diction in this piece—multiple modifiers filling the meter and terms like "bondsman" for "slave"—enacts the impulses toward generalization and cliché within the context of a specific communal history—an embodied history—within America. These contradictory impulses, found less self-consciously throughout the work of other elocutionists, inform the most global aspect of Brown's transformation of that theory, her explicit articulation of the social and moral purpose of elocution theory.

"Bound by the Strong Law of Obligation": Social Responsibility as a Pedagogical Construct in *Bits and Odds*

In contrast to other elocutionary theorists, Brown bases her pedagogical choices on a politicized course of study for an African American audience. Her emphasis on the linguistic heritage and cultural history of African Americans fuels her third pedagogical purpose, which is to instill a sense of social responsibility in those who gain elocutionary expertise. By making language and history such important components of her elocutionary curriculum, Brown foregrounds the relationship between the development of cultural pride and social and political action. While rhetorical instruction in the eighteenth and nineteenth centuries was well known for its promotion of taste and moral purpose, Brown joined those pedagogues who emphasized the development of a moral consciousness over an aesthetic one. In *The Peerless Speaker*, for example, Frank H. Fenno explains that "an improved style will suggest better thoughts, and as so much of our happiness if not existence itself depends upon a conveyance of our ideas, cultivation in this direction will certainly make us happier, nobler, and better." Another important elocutionary theorist of the period, S. S. Curry points out elocution's role in the development of taste, adding that it provides a "means for the development of the human being" (qtd. in Johnson, "Popularization" 150).

However, in many popular turn-of-the-century elocutionary treatises, theorists such as J. W. Shoemaker draw attention to moral transformation as the primary benefit of rhetorical study:

> It is only the *voice* that has reached its best, and the *eye* that beams from the *soul*, and the *hand* of *grace*, and the *attitude* of *manhood* and *womanhood*, that can convey the immortality which has been breathed upon us. By sin these powers have been enfeebled and deformed and under its burden their deformity increases. Guarded and regulated by the laws of our creation, they may be rescued and made potential in conveying the very mind of the Creator. (17)

Excerpts such as this one were very common in authors' introductions to elocution manuals, frequently highlighting the moral benefits of elocutionary study. Such benefits, however, are often advertised in the spirit of sanctimonious self-improvement; that is to say, they promote personal gain over community service. Consider this excerpt from the preface of *Delsarte Sys-*

tem of Oratory that accents the individual attention offered to those who speak powerfully:

> Orators, you are called to the ministry of speech. You have fixed your choice upon the pulpit, the bar, the tribune or the stage. You will become one day, preacher, advocate, lecturer or actor; in short, you desire to embrace the orator's career. I applaud your design. You will enter upon the noblest and most glorious of vocations. . . . While we award praise and glory to great musicians and painters, to great masters of sculpture and architecture, the prize of honor is decreed to great orators. (xxiii)

In drawing attention to oratory as "the most glorious of vocations," the author of this preface situates elocutionary practice in a context of personal gain. In this respect, oratory is promoted as a means to individual glory and fame—the kind afforded to musicians, painters, and sculptors.

Brown, on the other hand, emphasizes elocutionary study within her texts not for the sake of individual moral sanctity or personal acclaim, but for the shaping of a wide social vision and what the NACW often referred to as the "social uplift" of African Americans. This emphasis extends the tradition of many popular elocution theorists by broadening the focus from individual sanctity and self-improvement to a devotion to community. For if "taste" is always described in elocutionary theory in terms of its possession by an individual, Brown makes "moral strength" a quality that manifests itself globally in social action. In this way she transforms her own elocutionary theory to emphasize the communal possibilities gained through individual elocutionary study.

Emphasizing the connection between elocution and the development of social consciousness, Brown distinguishes herself from other mainstream elocutionary theorists who were more likely to stress the habits of mind that would separate the person schooled in elocution from a less educated citizenry. In her estimation, elocutionary study promised much for the African American community, for Brown argues that those educated in elocutionary principles would be inspired to help those less fortunate. Observing that elocution "gives mental and moral strength, great power, and a wide social influence to all who will take the time and patience to master it" ("First Lessons" 171), Brown stresses that intellect, void of character and empathy for others, is less valuable than intellect embodied in community concern:

> The intellect is highly trained in our schools and institutions of learning, but little or no regard is paid to the systematic training of the higher powers. . . . intellect is not the highest gift to man. The business of intellect is simply to know. Above and back of that stands character—the soul that di-

rects and impels both mind and body. Elocution teaches the student that he is to cultivate these higher powers; that he is to quicken his sense of obligation to himself, to his fellow man. . . . (165)

Brown establishes a relationship between learning how to deliver a message and carrying a message of service to others that is quite remarkable in its repetition throughout her work. Out of her intense belief in the transformative power of elocution and its relationship to "the systematic training of the higher powers," Brown writes of the responsibility educated individuals have to address the needs of the larger community.

Suggesting in her elocution and reciter texts that the study of elocution aligns the mind and the body with a spiritual purpose, Brown consistently urges those who progress intellectually to pass that knowledge on:

> When we have mastered these difficulties and made ourselves proficient, we are bound by the strong law of *Obligation.* Obligation to the man who is down. The vision and the cry from Macedonia are as real and vivid today as they were to the Apostle Paul—They come from those who sit in darkness, not only in foreign field, but at our very door—from the delta, canebrake, cotton field and rice swamp. ("Not Gifts" 176)

Raised in the African Methodist Episcopal Church, Brown's own upbringing and background, it appears, made it difficult for her to forget those in "the delta, canebrake, cotton field and rice swamp." Indeed, her activist and religious upbringing later affected the moral sense of the elocutionary theory she was to advocate. Given that her parents' home in Pennsylvania was a central meeting place for ministers, as well as a station for the Underground Railroad, it seems understandable that she would have forged an important relationship between oratorical culture and social activism.

Brown had, throughout her childhood, witnessed an alliance between the oral tradition of the pulpit and political goals. Indeed, within many of her texts, she invokes the religious ethos of a minister stressing the relationship between education and social responsibility:

> Be prepared to carry the message. Give up the pleasure of the *good time. Sacrifice!* Sacrifice elevates, service redeems a people. You will hear from time to time that your first duty is to get money, land and houses—to carve your name on the Scroll of Fame—to get learning so that you may have power to control men and measures. When you are obsessed with this idea—when you are carried on by this worldly ambition—the day you make such a choice, the Soul with you dies! ("First Lessons in Public Speaking," qtd. in McFarlin 176)

Such calls to social consciousness were certainly not present in mainstream elocutionary texts that promoted elocutionary theory by emphasizing the potential economic and social rewards that could be obtained by the individual skilled speaker. Brown, unlike popular theorists such as Curry and Shoemaker, makes no mention of the connection between elocutionary study and economic gain. Instead, she stresses again and again the importance of the social responsibilities of the educated. By infusing her materials with activist intent, Brown prepared not only to educate a certain constituency, but to mobilize that constituency for political action.

In many ways, Brown's views in this regard resonate with those of a more contemporary educator, Paulo Freire, who helped launch a massive literacy campaign in Brazil in the 1960s as he came to understand how traditional education failed to meet the needs of disenfranchised people. Crafting a literacy program for disempowered peasants, Freire and his students implemented a form of activist education that encouraged participants to intervene productively in an oppressive political system.

Freire's work insists that the achievement of literacy for marginalized students should not fuse education and capitalistic individualism; it argues that the primary purpose of education must be social consciousness:

> It is essential for the oppressed to realize that when they accept the struggle for humanization they also accept, from that moment, their total responsibility for the struggle. . . . The oppressed, who have been shaped by the death-affirming climate of oppression, must find through their struggle the way to life-affirming humanization, which does not lie *simply* in having more to eat. . . . (50)

What Freire calls "total responsibility" is what I describe as the "global" aspect of Brown's pedagogy. Like Freire, Brown recognized that social change could come only through an educational venture that extended its concerns beyond economic aspirations. As a result, it was imperative that her pedagogy confront the social purpose of elocutionary study and contextualize it in terms of the needs of the larger community. This pedagogical construct was, in many ways, the most remarkable of all of Brown's transformations of the traditional elocutionary theory, for by emphasizing social concerns, Brown politicized her course of study in a manner that no other mainstream elocutionist had before her, and she engaged the "Lifting as We Climb" principle that was so much a part of the black women's club movement at the turn of the century.

Brown's own affiliation with the NACW resulted in the opportunity to give a number of speeches and make many public appearances for the sake of educational advancement for blacks. She always saw the relationship between schooling and larger political gains as a symbiotic one. On the one hand, Brown recognized that African Americans would not be better off economically until they were better educated; however, she also realized that they would not have better educational opportunities until they made significant political gains. The following is an excerpt from a speech made by Brown during the time she served as a leader in the NACW:

> We believe that the right thinking White American will soon realize that he cannot afford to ignore twelve million loyal citizens of color. It is sadly true that unjust laws are enacted and cruel discriminations made against the Negro. He is held aloof by every other group forming a part of this nation. He is regarded by many as a liability rather than an asset in promoting the value of American life. . . . The colored man does not want *Negro domination* and is always opposed to *white supremacy.* He asks for a fair chance in life to own and control his home wherever he is able to establish and maintain it. He asks for the opportunity guaranteed every other loyal, public spirited citizen to send his children to schools as well equipped and open the same number of months as those attended by any other group of children. ("Not Gifts" 180)

This speech enlists a theme that Brown often emphasized—the effects of racism on inferior educational opportunities. Here and elsewhere in her work, Brown courageously invokes terms such as "white supremacy" in her arguments to blatantly describe the abuses blacks endured in post–Civil War America. Drawing attention to the ways the African American "is held aloof by every other group forming a part of this nation" Brown alludes to the argument she made elsewhere in other writings that immigrants from other countries received the invitation to become American citizens in ways that blacks did not. She adds that the African American "is regarded by many as a liability rather than an asset in promoting the value of American life. . . ." To address the hostility toward African Americans that refused them an "American" identity, Brown resigned herself to the battle of preserving African American contributions and images in her performances, speeches, and the selections in her reciter text so that blacks would not subscribe to the negative stereotypes of them promoted elsewhere in a country that refused them any distinguished cultural heritage.

Embodied Rhetoric and the Ethics of Community

For those who did not have the opportunity to study rhetoric in a formal academy, Brown's works offered special promise. Not only did her texts provide a vehicle to obtain a form of education that was often denied to African Americans, but Brown's elocutionary materials exposed an African American audience to the literature that made use of its linguistic heritage and history. Such deviations from standard elocution pedagogy cannot be underestimated or minimized within the scope of the history of rhetorical instruction, for as rhetoric and composition scholars work increasingly to recover a history of writing and speaking instruction that existed outside the formal academy, it appears that numerous transformations of rhetorical instruction for disenfranchised students remain to be recovered.

The emergence of Black Studies, Women's Studies, and Cultural Studies ushers in a new intellectual climate, providing critics the opportunity to view a wide variety of cultural practices in terms of a politics of difference. Cornel West observes that this shifting critical moment is in the process of creating a new intellectual consciousness that seeks "to undermine the prevailing disciplinary divisions of labor in the academy, museum, mass media and gallery networks. . ." (19). This movement is largely responsible for a national reflection on the ideological nature of schooling and curricula, as educators, politicians, and policy makers find themselves immersed in one of the bitterest educational debates in history. While some may assume the debate over pedagogy and politics to be a relatively recent development, Brown's work suggests that sites of learning and education have, throughout history, embodied political implications and that curricula have often been generated within the scope of ideological concerns.

But Brown's work teaches us more about the questions and goals we bring to education in America. What is most striking about her work is the place of ethics that she sees within the embodied work of history and politics. Ethics for Brown defines community, and the language of obligation and responsibility she uses is at the heart of her conception of education. I might even say that the very embodiment of education for Brown, beyond "intelligence," "taste," and "discernment," is precisely the ethics of community. For Brown, linguistic education is social education: It embodies and preserves a history of community action—whether it be black soldiers fighting for their own freedom, as in George Baker's poem that Brown includes in *Bits and Odds* quoted above, or the barely remembered "Afric" community in Frances Harper's poem. Such a conception of "embodiment," enacted in her study and transformation of elocution and in her own life as an activist educator, offers an important lesson for us as we pursue a stronger understanding of the relationship among racial identity, community, and rhetorical instruction in our own time.

4

IDEOLOGY AND RHETORICAL INSTRUCTION: BROOKWOOD LABOR COLLEGE

> The labor movement is more and more a factor in democracy and if we hold to our slogan, "Education for Democracy," we shall have in some way to acknowledge that the labor movement is one of the most, if not the most important factors in progress. Education for democracy without education for service in the labor movement is presenting the play of Hamlet with Hamlet left out.
> —Josephine Colby, Brookwood Educator, 1922

> When labor strikes, it says to its master: I shall no longer work at your command. When it votes for a party of its own, it says: I shall no longer vote at your command. When it creates its own classes and colleges, it says: I shall no longer think at your command. Labor's challenge to education is the most fundamental of the three.
> —Henry de Man, *New Republic*, 1922

During the 1920s, a workers' education movement took hold all across the United States; in the years following World War I, labor colleges and workers' schools emerged in nearly every city in the nation. Brookwood Labor College, Commonwealth College, and the Wisconsin School for Women Workers were among those schools established by labor leaders and liberal intellectuals because of their conviction that mainstream education did not and could not address the needs of workers and their children. In 1921, James Mauer, socialist president of the Pennsylvania Federation of Labor and an advocate of workers' education had this to say of the capitalist curricular agenda in the United States:

Our children are being trained like dogs and ponies, not developed as individuals. Such methods, together with the vicious propaganda on social and economic questions to which the children are subjected, produce just the results that the conservative and reactionary want, namely uniformity of thought and conduct, no originality of self-reliance except for money-making schemes, a worshipful attitude toward those who have wealth and power, intolerance for anything that the business element condemns, and ignorance of the great social and economic forces that are shaping the destinies of all of us. (qtd. in Altenbaugh 77)

Many who shared Mauer's estimation of public education saw a need for the problem to be addressed by the labor movement. They wanted workers to understand how history, economics, literature, and language in the public system of education perpetuated the status quo in the United States and resulted in the exploitation of the American worker. Members of unions from a wide variety of industries supported workers' education and joined together to generate curricula that would help students to understand the culture of class and the capitalistic biases of education in America.

While a number of residential labor colleges opened their doors during the twenties and thirties, no labor college proved more successful in attracting large numbers of students and setting the tone for workers' education in America than Brookwood Labor College. Founded in Katonah, New York, this institution produced (between 1921 and 1937) more well-known labor leaders than any other school of its type. It boasted among its graduates Walter Reuther, who helped to organize the United Auto Workers; Joseph Ozanic, who became president of the Progressive Mine Workers of America; and Len De Caux, who was the publicity director of the AFL-CIO. Like other labor colleges such as Commonwealth College, Work People's College, and the Bryn Mawr School for Women Workers, Brookwood put a curriculum in place that aided student-workers in becoming labor activists who could effectively challenge the economic structure of the United States.

While the entire curriculum at Brookwood Labor College was intensely politicized in terms of labor interests, those courses that focused on language and the political implications of discourse illustrate how Brookwood disengaged itself from the project of American capitalism by privileging neither "standard English," a literary aesthetic defined by ruling-class codes, nor a capitalistic rationale for education. Students were asked to think about language and the ways it functions in a wide variety of contexts so that they might enlist their rhetorical skills in the service of the labor movement.

Three Brookwood educators—Josephine Colby, Helen Norton, and Louis Budenz—were keenly aware of the ways that rhetorical study could help student-workers to become more effective union organizers and, in that process, recruit more labor organizers. While their courses varied in approach to rhetorical principles (Colby taught public speaking, Norton taught labor journalism, and Budenz taught field work—a course in planning and enacting strikes), each of these educators was deeply committed to rhetorical education that would enable students to campaign against abhorrent working conditions and low wages through *public speaking, public writing,* and *public action.*

The relationship between the strategic use of language and political action has long been emphasized by political and rhetorical theorists; however, a specific reference to the connection between rhetoric and class revolution appears in Marx's *Eighteenth Brumaire.* In this excerpt he argues that without the shared awareness created through language, class distinctions fail to exist at all. "Insofar as millions of families live under economic conditions of existence that separate their mode of life," he writes, "they form a class. Insofar as . . . the identity of their interests fails to produce a feeling of community . . . they do not form a class" (124). The role of language in producing such a "feeling of community" must be emphasized here, for certainly it is discourse that shapes the understanding of group identity in any context and gives a group a sense of a shared mission or goals. In the case of the American labor movement and indeed in the example of Brookwood Labor College itself, workers could not be expected to mobilize their energies against the exploitive forces of industry without an awareness of shared interests communicated effectively through writing or speaking.

To create a community based on a shared understanding of class issues, Brookwood's founders proposed a curriculum offering student-workers a heightened sense of their location in the larger culture. The commitment Brookwood educators had to this student population enabled them to propose and teach classes that adhered to the features of rhetorical instruction identified throughout this study. These features manifested themselves in the pedagogical materials of Colby, Norton, and Budenz and consistently demonstrated (1) an acknowledgment of the strategic use of working-class vernacular, (2) a commitment to writing and speaking assignments promoting critical consciousness, and (3) an emphasis on rhetorical instruction for the sake of social responsibility. Such features of writing and speaking instruction did not typically appear in the curricula of more traditional institutions, as I will demonstrate later in this chapter. The politicization of rhetoric curricula at Brookwood worked to further the goals of the school, as well as those of the labor movement in general. Through curricula sharply politicized in terms of labor movement's interests, these educators emphasized the ideological nature of schooling in the ways they addressed the relationship between language and identity in their classrooms, in the assignments they gave their students that required them to examine class structure, and in the ways they stressed students should use their rhetorical expertise in service to the labor movement.

First of all, Colby, Norton, and Budenz made a place for the working person's vernacular in their classrooms because they recognized the important relationship between language and identity as it emerged in the writing and the speech of members of the working class. Although Brookwood educators instructed students in standard English, they urged them to recognize the strategic possibilities of using working-class vernacular in recruiting workers. In many instances, their pedagogical materials acknowledge the advantageous uses of a discourse that, by the standards of most colleges and universities, would simply have been deemed "incorrect." However, in the context of Brookwood and the labor movement, this discourse had special currency and was acknowledged for its usefulness in recruitment efforts.

My use of the term *working-class vernacular* is intended to cover a variety of language practices outside the dictates of standard English. Certainly members of the working class spoke and wrote in a variety of forms of English. Some may have spoken Yiddish-English or perhaps a combination of Italian dialect and broken English or numerous other hybrid forms of English outside the boundaries of what is commonly referred to as standard English. I emphasize educators' treatment of what I am calling working-class vernacular because it is significant that educators were not so willing as others may have been in more traditional colleges and universities to simply dismiss workers' ways of speaking and writing as incorrect. In other words, they saw a strategic use for the language that would be used to recruit other workers of similar backgrounds.

In addition to the attention given to working-class vernacular in rhetoric courses, Brookwood educators offered assignments to students that asked them to consider the many abuses endured by workers in America's mines, mills, and factories because they wanted to enhance the class consciousness of their students. Assignments in rhetoric courses at Brookwood required students to examine, in speaking and writing, the ways that poor working conditions and poor wages affected their own lives and the lives of others. Such consistent attention to these issues helped them to remember the cause to which they were committed and the ways in which the labor movement might help to end worker exploitation.

Finally, in their pedagogical materials, Colby, Norton, and Budenz emphasized education for social responsibility because of their conviction that rhetorical expertise should serve the labor movement instead of American capitalism. Throughout the materials that guided their study, Brookwood students were always expected to remember that they were being educated, not for individual economic gain, but for the purpose of an economic revolution that could serve the interests of all working-class people.

I wish, then, to examine these features of rhetorical instruction at Brookwood and to analyze how rhetorical study at this institution corresponds to other college writing and speaking courses in more traditional schools throughout the country at this time. My aim is to demonstrate how Brookwood's rhetoric curriculum proved more radical than curricula in more traditional institutions because the form of politicized language study at this school refused to promote the uncritical literacy education of the larger culture.

In addition to the investigation of politicized rhetorical education, I also note how issues of difference emerged in the institution and how racism, sexism, and religious prejudice challenged Brookwood's egalitarian goals to end class structure in the United States. Because this institution made no consistent attempt to address other issues of difference, they often worked against the primary mission of Brookwood, which was, of course, to address class inequalities. Ultimately, Brookwood's failure to confront them contributed to the demise of the institution. Later in the chapter I examine documents that reveal the complex dynamics in play among women, teachers and students, blacks, Jews, and other groups who attended or worked at Brookwood during the time it was one of the most well-known labor colleges in America.

The American Labor Movement and the Need for Liberatory Labor Education

Some overview of the social and political climate during which the labor colleges emerged may help to illustrate why a need for these institutions arose in the United States during the twenties and thirties. Certainly one of the most remarkable features of the labor colleges is that many of them were founded while the labor movement was under tremendous attack in the United States. For in the wake of the 1917 Bolshevik revolution in Russia, many Americans feared a similar revolution in the United States and sought to deter the kinds of sympathetic alliances that could provoke such an upheaval.[1] Due to a number of events that increased anti-labor sentiment, it became difficult to engage laborers in social protest during the 1920s. American workers continued to endure many hardships, however, and labor activists urged the unions to take an aggressive stance to protect the movement and the people it served. Some suggested that workers ought to be better educated in order to resist the exploitive practices of industrial employers and the government bureaucracy that sought to discourage union membership; as a result, a group of union members and liberal intellectuals began to envision an alternative form of education for members of the labor movement.

A worker's education conference was held in New York City in 1921 by labor leaders and liberal intellectuals to investigate the ways in which working-class culture might inform pedagogy at schools designed for workers. This important conference helped to make Brookwood's opening in the autumn of that same year possible.[2] One of the institution's primary founders, William Mann Fincke, was inspired by educational reformists such as John Dewey, who suggested the need for an educational revolution through the advocacy of student-centered pedagogies. The son of a wealthy coal operator, Fincke grew disillusioned after working briefly for his father. Entering the ministry and becoming a Christian Socialist, he spoke out against the church for its apathy to labor and social reform. Fincke and his wife Helen purchased an estate in rural Katonah, New York, in 1914 in hopes of creating a progressive labor college that could enact many of the ideas of Dewey and other reformist educators (Altenbaugh 70). According to Joyce Kornbluh, "Dewey's assertion that the *process* of a democratic education would lead to a democratic society became the maxim of adult educators in general, and workers' education leaders in particular." Kornbluh adds that Dewey's 1916 *Democracy and Education* had a considerable influence on the curricula and educational philosophy at Brookwood because it helped them to focus on four major principles of workers' education:

> (1) involving participants in developing curricula based on their own needs and interests; (2) opposing the isolation of schooling from the real world; (3) building learning experiences around real-life situations; and (4) viewing the education process as a means of social change. (14)

These defining features of workers' education, as the following sections of this chapter will demonstrate, formed the foundation of the rhetoric curriculum and helped to give other fields of study at Brookwood their particular ideological emphasis.

Moreover, these foundational concepts of workers' education are also evident in the mission statement of the college. A number of liberal intellectuals, including A. J. Muste, who became the school's director, worked with Fincke to create the following mission statement for the institution, a statement that characterizes Brookwood's radical socialist ideology:

> In determining courses, teaching methods, and all matters of educational policy, Brookwood asks one question: What can a resident school do to

enable American workers to work more effectively in the American labor movement? Brookwood is interested in the ultimate and spiritual aims of the labor movement, as well as in its immediate, material aims. It regards the labor movement not merely as a machine to secure higher wages, shorter hours, certain improved conditions in the shop, but as the most vital and noble force of our time working to bring a better life for all men. (Questionnaire)

This mission statement defined the political nature of a course of study that boasted such titles as *The Literature of Revolt, Labor Dramatics,* and *The History of the Workers in America,* as well as numerous other courses that reflected the ideology of the institution. Like so many labor colleges across the nation, Brookwood promoted a curriculum that could never be divorced from actual events in the labor struggle; classroom interaction was always interfaced with militant off-campus activities. This was particularly characteristic of rhetoric courses at Brookwood, where the study of language was carried out within the context of labor activism (Altenbaugh 92–93).

Education for Activism: Rhetorical Components of the Brookwood Curriculum

In rhetoric courses at Brookwood, students were encouraged to write, speak, and read their experiences from a critical perspective, in terms of historical and cultural particularities. The analysis of pedagogical materials in this chapter emphasizes the ways in which Colby, Norton, and Budenz asked students to see that culture is linked to power and how ruling class codes condition working-class students. As a result of this understanding, these educators designed courses that foregrounded the political implications of discourse in the workplace and in the labor movement itself. Helen Norton, who taught labor journalism, gives some indication of this pedagogical feature in this excerpt from her correspondence with other educators as she explains why students come to Brookwood to study rhetoric and other academic subjects contextualized in terms of labor interests:

They're coming, in the first place, for knowledge . . . knowledge about their own unions, about the history of the labor movement in this and other countries. . . . Then they're coming to learn how to use facts after they have them—how to express their ideals so the crowd will get them and be moved to *action* by them; how to put ideas into print so people will read and understand them. They're coming to learn how people act under given conditions and why, and all the other things that psychology can teach about handling groups and individuals. (qtd. in Altenbaugh 93)

Norton touches on a dimension of rhetoric studies that was first articulated by Aristotle and other classical rhetoricians who emphasized the relationship between communication and political outcomes. Norton's characterization of Brookwood students' motivation to learn "how people act under given conditions" highlights the relationship between politics and discourse and underscores the importance of rhetoric studies in the Brookwood curriculum.

Honoring Language and Identity: Working-Class Vernacular and the Rhetoric of Labor Movement Recruitment

I have suggested throughout this book that the modes of rhetorical instruction in mainstream institutions often failed to meet the needs of diverse student populations because, in most cases, these approaches did not respect the linguistic conventions of disenfranchised people, nor did they demonstrate an understanding of the important relationship between language and identity. Teachers of rhetoric courses at Brookwood recognized not only the ways in which certain kinds of "outlawed" discourse conventions articulate a particular reality that does not always translate into "standard American English," but also saw the connection between specific kinds of language use and a sense of self, which is to say that they understood that when other educators simply characterized working-class vernacular as "incorrect," they were reinforcing attitudes of cultural inferiority.

In the case of Helen Norton, who taught labor journalism, an understanding of the relationship between language and cultural identity manifests itself in her pedagogical materials as well as in her correspondence with other educators. The daughter of a Kansas machinist, Norton graduated from Kansas State Agricultural College and came to teach at Brookwood when she was twenty-eight. She prepared students to participate in the labor movement through an increased awareness of rhetorical principles in practice, teaching students how to create and maintain a labor press as well as how to write leaflets, keep minutes, and write resolutions and reports. Norton established *The Brookwood Review,* a publication drawing heavily on the experiences of Brookwood students in various industrial sites as well as in the labor college community.

In a document advising students how to set up "shop papers," as they were called, Norton exhibits an awareness of the ways that language conventions create a sense of workers' solidarity. Underscoring the strategic nature of working-class language, Norton urges students to avoid "academic discourse" in order to be more effective in their recruitment efforts:

Keep the style of your paper intimate. Write about "us workers" rather than "you workers" or "the workers." Comb all the specialized ideologic phraseology out of your vocabulary and translate Marx into the thought and habit patterns of the locality. . . . Encourage workers to write up their experiences and ideas for the paper. . . . Don't cut and polish letters beyond recognition, and above all, don't twist them from their original intent. ("Shop Papers" 1)

Norton cautions students founding labor presses not to copy the expensive, elaborately illustrated company publications, noting that "many groups abandon the printed magazine or paper altogether and issue mimeographed papers whose very crudeness is effective" ("Shop Papers" 1). By emphasizing the influence of working-class culture on public relations campaigns down to the communicative features of typesetting and paper quality, Norton foreshadows the proclamation of media theorists such as Marshall McLuhan who, decades later, argued that the medium can never be divorced from the message itself (McLuhan 7).

Like the strategic use of simple "mimeographed papers whose very crudeness" Norton found to be rhetorically effective, the strategic nature of working-class vernacular and its relationship to communal action is an idea that surfaces again and again throughout her directions for founding shop papers. In a document that draws from the experiences of other former students who describe their successes enacting the principles of Labor Journalism, she includes, for instance, the words of a man who founded the *Cleaver,* a periodical designed to organize butcher workmen. The student writes:

I find the greatest temptation is to get literary and write masterpieces. But the members will save you from that. They're likely to say, "That was damned good, but it don't mean a thing to the butcher business." I know of no editing that requires more care—or that brings more results. ("Shop Papers" 2)

By foregrounding this advice from former students, Norton demonstrates again the power of working-class vernacular to define community within the labor movement and to generate action among workers. Promoting this form of discourse over a more polished academic discourse, she and her students acknowledged the capacity of such conventions to create workers' solidarity—a solidarity that could not be established through more "standard" forms of writing. Take, for example, the excerpt that utilizes colloquialisms such as "get literary," and "it don't mean a thing to the butcher business." Such phrases, commonly included in many of the student responses to assignments, indicate the ways in which working-class vernacular was used to create camaraderie among workers. It is worth noting, too, that for the author of this piece, any writer who wants to "get literary" runs the risk of failing to reach a majority of workers, even if he or she succeeds in writing "a masterpiece," for the goal of any shop paper is to create community—not to gain attention for an individualized aesthetic.

While Norton's Labor Journalism course offered practical information on writing articles for labor newspapers, Louis Budenz's field work course gave students a sense of the rhetorical history of the labor movement, as well as an understanding of how rhetorical principles related to audience. An attorney who acted as editor of the socialist periodical *Labor Age* before coming to Brookwood, Budenz taught courses well known for their anti-capitalist ideology. In the Brookwood course catalogue, for example, Field Work is described as "an analysis of strike situations and organizing campaigns; . . . making social surveys of localities; soap boxing tactics; publicity methods; problems of cooperation among different labor groups" (Altenbaugh 62). The goal of Field Work was to help students carry out successful strike campaigns; consequently, Budenz's classes provided extensive consideration of rhetorical strategies used throughout the labor movement's rich history—a history that notes the important role played by working-class vernacular.

Budenz urged his students to consider a work force in America composed of many people of different nationalities and cultural backgrounds. The organization of such a diverse group of people was an immense task, and the future of organized labor depended very much on workers' abilities to assess and respond to particular rhetorical situations. An understanding of how specific rhetorical strategies had failed or succeeded in strikes was crucial. Here, in an essay written for Budenz's field work course entitled "Problems of the Organizer," a Brookwood student named James Dick describes one rhetorical occasion all organizers were likely to encounter, a situation created by orthodox religion. Dick's response to Budenz's assignment to describe a particular problem of labor organizers communicates the crucial importance of knowing one's audience:

> Men and women have made mistakes because they did not understand the psychology of these people, but had certain opinions of their own and tried to tell them what they ought to think. These workers are very religious. I've ridden in strikers' cars and seen a Madonna on the radiator cap. What was that for? They couldn't get into an accident with the Madonna on the car. . . . You may be as irreligious as you like, but you can't get away with it on the public platforms.
> *The Approach to the Priest.* You may go to hell in your own way for all I care, but when you get into a mill town or a strike situation in which 99

percent of the people are Roman Catholics, you've got to deal with the priest. If you don't, he'll deal with you. The first priest I came in contact with in a strike was an Irishman, one of my own nationality. He was a tough old baby—a pacifist. He hated the British government so he fought against the United States going to war to help her. Someone told him I was a Bolshevik—this was when the Red raids were going on all over the country. He sent word to me he wanted to see me. We had quite an argument. I agreed with him that England was a bum country and that we oughtn't go to war to help her. At the first mass on the following Sunday he delivered a speech from the altar that I never would have dared deliver myself, denouncing strikebreakers and scabs. He refused to baptize their children, he refused to marry them, he refused to bury them. That man was wonderful in helping the strike.

If this student paper is similar to others produced by other students in this course, it illustrates the kind of assignments students received, assignments that required them to analyze modes of communication used in strikes for the purpose of improving similar campaigns in the future. It is significant that this excerpt from a student essay examines language and communication practices that proved successful as well as unsuccessful in a strike campaign. This student clearly understands the importance of organized religion to his audience. He insists, "You've got to deal with the priest. If you don't, he'll deal with you." Moreover, the composition indicates the student's understanding that working-class vernacular might succeed in situations where standard English might fail. Consider how this excerpt, like the student excerpt cited earlier, makes use of colloquialisms such as "tough old baby" and "bum country" to enact a particular informality that could be useful in a community where more formal English might serve to alienate potential members of the labor constituency.

These features of Norton's and Budenz's courses are particularly interesting because they acknowledge the importance of unsanctioned linguistic conventions for their strategic use in other contexts. Drawing sharp distinctions between "correct" and "incorrect" English, most texts used in academies throughout the country insisted on current-traditional principles that informed so many composition and rhetoric texts in the United States at this time. This insistence, as Berlin notes, resulted partially from the effect of scientific principles on pedagogical debates and from the belief that writing and speaking could be taught by developing the understanding of certain universal features of human behavior. This perspective lends another view to the influence of progressive educational theorists such as Dewey. Berlin observes, in fact, that "Most educators were not followers of Dewey . . . the respect for science led to a faith in Thorndike's contention that any feature of human behavior could be quantified, measured, and controlled" (*Rhetoric and Reality* 59). Noting the ways in which the application of empirical methods to the study of human behavior shaped pedagogical models during the progressive era, Berlin defines these competing models and sometimes conflicting methods of applying science to the education of young people, even as such methods sought to insist on students' individual differences.

Citing an extensive study by Warner Taylor conducted in 1927 and 1928, Berlin explains that of the 225 institutions across the nation that Taylor surveyed, the required texts for most rhetoric courses emphasize teaching students to produce documents that were grammatically correct but failed to provide the kind of philosophical language study that was so much a part of the Brookwood rhetoric curriculum (62–63).[3] In other words, such courses did not take up issues such as how nonstandard English might function in certain contexts or how particular speeches had succeeded or failed to motivate certain constituencies at specific historical moments. Most forms of rhetorical instruction in mainstream colleges and universities, as noted earlier, simply ignored the influence of culture on communication.[4] In light of the fact that rhetoric courses at most other academic institutions created such a strong distinction between "correct" and "incorrect" language, it seems even more remarkable that rhetoric teachers such as Norton and Budenz engaged the strategic possibilities of working-class vernacular in other contexts and made this feature a part of the rhetoric curriculum at Brookwood.

Politicized Writing and Speaking Assignments

While an awareness of the strategic possibilities of working-class vernacular was a feature of the Brookwood rhetoric curriculum, so, too, were writing and speaking assignments that urged students to consider their location in the larger culture. Colby, Norton, and Budenz assigned writing and speaking projects that required students to analyze the effects of poor wages, poor working conditions, and poorly organized working communities on their lives and the lives of others. Assignments such as these call to mind a term used by Paulo Freire and other contemporary activist educators to describe the process of education for "critical consciousness." Freire defines critical consciousness as an awareness generated by a particular kind of politicized curriculum and teaching methods:

> This pedagogy makes oppression and its causes objects of reflection by the
> oppressed, and from that reflection will come their necessary engagement

in the struggle for their liberation. And in the struggle this pedagogy will be made and remade. (*Pedagogy* 30)

Josephine Colby appears to have remade public speaking pedagogy in her courses by linking the assignments to, not only the labor movement, but the lives of student-workers. Colby, a former high school teacher and organizer for the American Federation of Teachers, taught public speaking courses designed to prepare students to become articulate union organizers. Her assignments required students to choose topics that related directly to problems of the laborer such as "What Good Wages Would Mean to Me" and "What Unemployment Did to a Village." Such assignments anticipated Freire's position that intensive consideration of these issues would aid students in gaining the "necessary engagement in the struggle for their liberation."

Although Colby relied on traditional public speaking pedagogy such as voice exercises, the ideological allegiance to the labor movement in such exercises is quite apparent. Students recited passages from Mary Heaton Vorse's "Strike" and other forms of labor-conscious literature such as the following poem by Robert Whitecar:

> Begging for bread—in a plentiful land;
> Begging for bread—with a trade in his hand.
> Sound as a dollar in heart and in head,
> Ready for work and yet begging for bread.
>
> Begging for bread—but not begging alone;
> Now are they swollen to numbers unknown;
> Who weary the highways with heart-breaking tread,
> And swarm through city streets—begging for bread.
>
> Begging for bread with such stores on our hands
> We could feed the unified of all habited lands;
> Food rotted to order—starvation widespread—
> Organized waste—millions begging for bread.
>
> Begging for bread while the dividends still
> Choke the fat coffers and bulge dives' till;
> "Coming-out parties" increasing their spread,
> And blessed in their name who are begging for bread.
>
> Chief of the nation today on the air,
> And all the big talkers with language to spare,

Urging the half-poor already well bled
To save our prosperity—begging for bread.

(Colby, Course Materials)

In addition to poems such as this one that emphasize the suffering of economic hardship, Colby's course packet utilized excerpts from speeches by John L. Lewis and other militant voices from the labor campaign. Colby's materials included numerous literary models in her courses for the sake of recitation practice; however, each of them emphasized the interests of the labor movement.

With this approach, Colby worked to enact the kind of critical reflection described by Freire in *Pedagogy of the Oppressed* and so many of his other works written about class struggle advanced through critical literacy. Freire stresses that in his own experience working with the people of Brazil:

> What was needed was to go to the people and help them to enter the historical process critically. The prerequisite for this task was a form of education enabling the people to reflect on themselves, their responsibilities, and their role in the new cultural climate—indeed to reflect on their very *power* of reflection. The resulting development of this power would mean an increased capacity for choice. (*Education* 16)

The forms of rhetorical education at Brookwood correspond to Freire's concept of "critical consciousness," as this overview of the curriculum illustrates; for the study of language was designed to help students to contemplate their own working experience in relation to that of others. This emphasis is particularly evident in assignments that asked students to reflect on their lives in America's mills and factories.

Colby, for example, valued the employment experiences of her students and stressed early in every course she taught that "The first work to be done is to learn to tell a story effectively" (Course Materials). This may be one reason for the presence of so many literary sources in her course materials. Berlin points to the increasing use of literature in most rhetoric courses during this time, as it was believed that literature trained students in the science of reading and writing (70–71). While Colby did not break with the more traditional conventions in this respect, her course materials do suggest the strong ideological nature of her courses and demonstrate the ways in which labor-conscious literature promoted the spirit of the institution.

The notebooks of Joseph Ozanic, a Brookwood student who later became president of the Progressive Mine Workers of America, provide a glimpse of rhetorical instruction at Brookwood from the student's perspective. The notebooks, which span a period from December 1930 to April

1931, contain Ozanic's detailed notes for all his courses, particularly public speaking. They show that Colby's public speaking students were encouraged to prepare speeches that could be delivered to potential union members, thus providing a realistic context for the assignments. Students were also asked to summarize works that were written by others on labor issues. On January 12, 1931, for example, Ozanic records in his notebook this assignment given by Colby:

> How would you go about writing a summary on industrialism from this essay of Bertrand Russell?
> 1) How could you write a short summary?
> 2) How could you make summaries of different lengths?
> Write a summary of the essay by B.R. [Bertrand Russell] in ten sentences.

The ability to take material from other complex sources and make it accessible to others was quite an important feature of Colby's courses, for students could realistically expect to be called on to speak extemporaneously on a wide variety of topics during recruitment efforts. Indeed, they might also be called to speak to groups of people with less education, and so it was crucial that students learn to summarize effectively. Exercises such as this one demonstrate one of the ways that they developed this skill even as such assignments required them to contemplate their cultural location in the process.

In addition to summarizing the work of more established writers and speakers, students learned to critique the work of their peers as they practiced speeches that might someday be given in the larger context of union recruitment events. Such assignments always helped students to receive crucial information that could be incorporated into actual recruitment efforts and did a great deal to encourage class consciousness, which was always a goal of educators at Brookwood.

Other evidence suggests that Brookwood educators encouraged students to obtain a deeper understanding of their own cultural location through assignments that focused on labor issues and working-class life experiences. This student essay, written for Helen Norton's labor journalism course, illustrates the important role that employment autobiographies played in the rhetoric curriculum. Employment autobiographies required students to examine the alienation and hardship that was all too often part of their lives and the lives of those workers they hoped to serve. Characteristic of many similar pieces published in the *Brookwood Review*, this student essay highlights the dangers to workers who labor without the support and protection of unions:

In to-and-fro light the looming mill toyed with rolling, white-hot tons of steel. The ingots looked melty-fringed, squeezable. The manipulators gesticulated, clasped the ingots, handled them, made the iron building shake. Thuddy echoes bumped about. Men nodded sleepily, and just before dawn a youngster screamed "Don't tell Mamma!" as he was crushed to death beneath a hydraulic accumulator. The hours were too long, twelve of them, seven days a week. . . . Money seemed to be the trouble. Without money, I cannot establish a residence, I cannot become a citizen of any community. Citizenship is gone. Without money, I may not be still. Automatically I find myself on the road, searching out the remotest construction job or harvest task, necessarily willing to work for any pay, or even board and room. But each community reserves such work for its own citizens. . . . Twenty-four hours is the time limit in each town. I am harassed, pursued, unwanted. Local authorities insist that I shall be fingerprinted. If I object—who am I? A potential criminal. (Shadduck 3–5)

Though it was probably not this student's intent to emphasize the need for community within the labor movement, it turns out nevertheless to be an underlying theme in this essay. This particular excerpt emphasizes the lack of status of the unemployed and the danger posed to individual lives when exploited workers have no sense of community. What happens to those individuals who cannot become part of a community defined solely by financial resources? This writer suggests that "Without money, I cannot establish a residence, I cannot become a citizen of any community." Indirectly, this student composition contrasts the need for workers' solidarity built on the interests of those who have been exploited in the enterprise of American capitalism.

Thus, through assignments requiring students to examine their work experience and their position in a society defined by material goods and financial resources, Norton, Budenz, and Colby's student work demonstrates how education for class consciousness proved to be a primary aspect of the rhetoric curriculum at Brookwood. The nature of these writing and speaking assignments emphasize the kind of personal interrogation of life experience educators at Brookwood demanded of their students so that they might not forget how their own experience tied them to the labor cause. In this educational context, it was crucial that students not forget where they came from after they received an education.

Rhetorical Instruction for Social Responsibility

Education for social responsibility became a central pedagogical construct, not just in rhetoric courses but throughout the entire curriculum at Brookwood. The school's mission statement indicates the expectations of union sponsors and Brookwood faculty that students would not be educated out of their social class, but would instead return to industry as active union organizers. About 10 percent of Brookwood's student population attended other colleges or universities after leaving Brookwood, but there are no statistics that show how many left the labor movement after achieving educational goals (J. Bloom 75).

Once students gained admission to the institution, reminders of the expectations for service to the movement upon graduation were woven into the fabric of the courses, and the rhetoric courses of Colby, Norton, and Budenz were no exception. While one of the primary goals of these courses was to graduate students who would be effective writers and speakers, the expectation was that rhetorical training was to be used, not to make money or gain employment outside the factory or mine, but to aid others whose exploitation might surpass their own. The responsibility of student-workers to serve the movement is a point that Brookwood's director, A. J. Muste, makes again and again:

> Brookwood is an integral part of the American labor movement and exists only to serve it. Its graduates go back to mine, mill and shop, and to their unions, not to get something out of the movement, but to put something into it, not to get jobs but to do work. This spirit of complete, practical devotion to the movement is the spirit of Brookwood. (Questionnaire)

Assignments in rhetoric courses at Brookwood worked to generate a sense of critical consciousness in student-workers as the previous section demonstrates; however, such assignments were also fused with the goals of social responsibility. For example, one of the ways that Colby, Norton, and Budenz succeeded in instilling a concern for others in their rhetoric curricula was to ask students to speak and write about the difficulties of others who had less power and education, those individuals whose interests Brookwood graduates were expected to serve when they left the institution.

Colby's topics for public speaking are a prime example of this strategy; she often encouraged students to examine the exploitation of others and to compare it to their own. Like the employment autobiographies, writing and speaking about the exploitation of others illustrated the dangers that come to people who fail to create a community, who fail to mobilize themselves for political action. In a model outline for the topic of "What Unemployment Did to a Family," Colby suggests the following headings:

Introduction: (How the Family used to Stand in the Community)
   I. What Unemployment Did to the Wage-earners.
   II. What it Did to the Children.

Assignments such as this one were designed to turn the attention of workers away from their own victimization and to mobilize their energies to help others with fewer resources.

The Ozanic notebooks mentioned earlier contain evidence of the ways in which this pedagogical construct wove itself throughout the Brookwood curriculum. In class notes (again taken in Colby's public speaking course), Ozanic records excerpts from a classmate's speech entitled "Cooperation":

[T]he labor movement ought to be defined by the theory that mutual aid and not competition is the fundamental law of life, that the individual best serves his own interests by serving the interests of others with each for all and all for each as the guiding maxim of workers' society.

Like Jordan's call to her women students to remember women from other social classes who were exploited in textile mills and Brown's cry to never forget those in the delta and the swamp, this student emphasizes the maxim that was so much a part of this curriculum, that rhetorical instruction that failed to be used in the service of others, particularly in the service of exploited communities of people, was wasted. This idea, so central to the curriculum at institutions committed to serving disenfranchised students, insisted on the social change that might result from service. It should come as no surprise, then, given the nature of the mission statement of this institution and the assignments provided to students that this theme should surface in student work and in pedagogical materials again and again, for it was clearly one of the guiding forces of the institution.

The Challenge of Political, Ideological, and Cultural Diversity at Brookwood

Despite this emphasis on service, however, a number of problems challenged this ideal within the labor movement and within this particular labor college itself. The failure of the labor movement and the failure of the labor college curriculum to consider how other issues of difference threatened their primary goals ultimately made the institution less effective and finally contributed to its demise. The plight of the American laborer was not always enough to unite this diverse community of student-workers. This fact was acknowledged in the *Twelfth Anniversary Review*, a Brookwood publication:

Some years ago a miner from the Middle West, looking over his fellow students for the first time asked, "What are these Jewish girls doing here? There ain't no Jews in the labor movement." The needle trades unions were completely unknown to him and he was even more surprised when the girls not only outshone him on labor theory—of which, in truth, he had very little—

but even in discussion of tactics on which he considered himself an authority. The girls, too, soon had to revise their opinion of the miner and acknowledge that lack of sophistication did not betoken hopeless ignorance.

This incident and others suggest that issues of difference among Brookwood students challenged the school's best intentions at times. Ironically, although Brookwood faculty and students criticized the AFL for discriminating against black and female workers and stated that they did not want to perpetuate the racist and sexist power relations of that organization, Brookwood was not untainted by similar prejudices.

While overt accounts of underlying racism and sexism are difficult to locate, there is evidence that this labor college community was affected by issues of ethnicity and gender. In terms of admission alone, the numbers are telling. Although foreign-born whites made up 31.7 percent of Brookwood's student population between 1921 and 1931, few blacks, in fact, were ever admitted to Brookwood: During the same ten-year period, only five African Americans attended this labor college, accounting for less than 1 percent of the overall student population. While a multitude of unions and other organizations provided scholarships for white and foreign-born students to attend Brookwood, scholarships for African Americans were provided only by the National Association for the Advancement of Colored People and the Sleeping Car Porters. The demographic composition of Brookwood is curious indeed in light of the institution's accusations of racism in the AFL and the mission statement of Brookwood itself, which claimed that "the labor and farmer movements constitute the most vital concrete force working for human freedom and . . . they can bring in a new era of justice and human brotherhood" (Report on Brookwood Activities).

Although women comprised nearly 40 percent of the student population at Brookwood, most of the labor leaders who were educated at Brookwood and achieved prominent leadership positions in the labor movement were men. While male labor leaders (and Brookwood graduates) such as John Brophy, William Green, and Len De Caux speak fondly of the school in their biographies and autobiographies, female labor activists (and Brookwood alumni) such as Peggy Dennis, Rose Pesotta, and Constance Ashton Myers are notably silent on this subject and make no mention of ever attending Brookwood at all. This silence in itself is curious and suggests that these and other women may have experienced Brookwood as another kind of learning environment entirely.

Len De Caux, who later became publicity director of the CIO, reveals some sense of how women may have been perceived by their male "comrades" at Brookwood.[5] In his autobiography, De Caux devotes several pages to the women he knew while he was a student at the labor college. Although he claims to admire the extraordinary new breed of female student at Brookwood, a patronizing tone bleeds through De Caux's sexist account of such women:

> Brookwood had some women students of "leadership caliber"—that is, of matronly composure and stable build, loyal to union leaders who sponsored them. It also had centrists who didn't enjoy factional hair-pulling and being bitter against the left, but for whom the left was too far out for respectability. But the lefties fascinated me most. These were among the younger and prettier girls—not a virago among them. They were lively, enthusiastic, emotional—shedding many a tear when Lenin died. (105)

De Caux describes a number of the women whom he dated during his Brookwood days, stressing above all that women at Brookwood were "Politically active . . . inspired by humanistic aims and a world-ranging revolutionary philosophy. And they were feminine" (106). Although De Caux praises many of his female acquaintances at Brookwood for their "brains, practicality, and labor experience," many of the accolades he delivers are undermined by his statement that such admirable qualities were "all wrapped up in one trim, sweet pretty package" (106). One might speculate how sentiments such as those conveyed here by De Caux may have affected women, even in an idealistic and somewhat utopian educational environment such as Brookwood. De Caux's indication that the best female labor radicals were "pretty," "feminine," and never scolding or scornful is certainly problematic when viewed in relation to the atmosphere of equality the school espoused.

The Closing of Brookwood and the Effects of the Workers' Education Movement

Over the years, tensions increased between Brookwood Labor College and the American Federation of Labor due to the alienation of the AFL by Brookwood faculty and students who published articles accusing the powerful organization of ignoring women, ethnic minorities, and workers in various trades, particularly textiles. On the other hand, Brookwood's reformist vision for confronting issues of difference within the labor movement found no support among AFL leaders. Despite the best efforts of Brookwood educators to create a practical, useful climate for workers' education, according to Richard Altenbaugh, "Critics saw the schools as elitist, expensive, and out of touch with the farm and workplace" (222–23). Brookwood's pastoral location in rural Katonah, away from the factories of New York

City helped to fuel this notion. The AFL began to describe Brookwood and other labor colleges in "ivy-league" terms, stressing that labor colleges were increasingly removed from the problems of the American worker.

In addition to these difficulties, Brookwood faculty and students began to split into various factions, divided over issues such as whether violence should be used in strikes or whether Brookwood should remain estranged from the AFL. A. J. Muste, the school's director, took a great deal of criticism from both the right and the left. In 1928, Matthew Woll, an AFL official, accused Brookwood of demonstrating "anti-religious" and "red tendencies." He rallied the AFL against Brookwood at the same time as Marxists criticized Muste for the opposite reason. This faction suggested that Muste was not radical enough, that he fired left-wing scholars from teaching posts and expelled students who agreed with the ideology of communism (Myers 72–73). These factors, combined with the desperate economic times during the depression, resulted in dwindling funds for workers' education, and Brookwood, like all other labor colleges, suffered. As a result of these conflicts, monetary support for the institution declined. Unfortunately, Brookwood depended on union scholarships to support the students who attended the college.

Eventually, in late 1937, Brookwood Labor College was forced to close its doors. The economic climate of the country, combined with the anti–labor college sentiment within the AFL took its toll. Although professors went without pay for a year and the college made other kinds of financial sacrifices, it was not enough. After sixteen years of serving workers from a wide variety of backgrounds, Brookwood Labor College closed and did not open again.

While the college was not successful in its ultimate goal of a true social revolution, it is clear that a number of Brookwood graduates went on to assume prominent leadership positions. Charles Howlett notes that the *Biographical Dictionary of American Labor Leaders,* a who's who in the field, lists more faculty and students from Brookwood than from any other college in the nation (332).

Twelve years after its founding, at a celebration in New York to commemorate the college, this tribute was paid to the faculty and former students of Brookwood:

> Whether it be among the textile workers in the South and New England or among the steel workers of Ohio and Pennsylvania, in needle trades centers from New York to Los Angeles, in workers' education classes in West Virginia or Colorado, in writing for the labor press or in the cooperative movement, in powerful unions like the Hosiery Workers or struggling new

unions like the Progressive Miners of Illinois, in working for the release of Tom Mooney or for the economic freedom of the Negro, fighting racketeering in the unions or forming unemployed leagues, there Brookwooders are to be found putting into practice the precepts they learned at this labor school and—more important—bringing the labor movement a contagious idealism and fervor. (*Twelfth Anniversary Review*)

Though it is difficult to measure the ultimate achievements of a labor college with an activist rhetoric curriculum such as Brookwood, this much should be observed: During the period of 1921–1937, rhetoric professors at Brookwood Labor College designed and taught courses that challenged public education's privileged ideological terrain in the spirit of a movement that had important results for the labor movement as a whole. By emphasizing students' working-class experiences and by teaching students to view that experience from a critical perspective, progressive rhetoric instructors at Brookwood helped to shape a community of future labor leaders and activists. Reading, writing, and speaking about their employment experiences gave Brookwood students the opportunity to gain a critical perspective on the forces that threatened their lives and well-being.

Brookwood Labor College provided an ideal site for enacting a liberatory curriculum devoted to rhetorical study. Students and faculty worked together to bring better wages and working conditions to America. Adult and nontraditional students found respect in a community that celebrated working-class culture, even in the face of other challenges posed by race, sex, and labor ideologies. Though a common goal was not ultimately enough to sustain this community, for a time students had the opportunity to participate in a labor movement that needed their vision, their wisdom, and their rhetorical expertise in the struggle against economic exploitation in the industrial workplace.

5

BORDERLANDS, INTERSECTIONS, AND ONGOING HISTORY: RHETORIC AND ACTIVISM IN HIGHER EDUCATION

To anyone who is sensitive to the radical dissimilarity of our present to all past situations, the study of the past "as an end in itself" can only appear as thoughtless obstructionism, as willful resistance to the attempt to close with the present world in all its strangeness and mystery. In the world in which we daily live, anyone who studies the past as an end in itself must appear either an antiquarian, fleeing from the problems of the present into a purely personal past, or a kind of cultural necrophile, that is, one who finds in the dead and dying a value he can never find in the living. The contemporary historian has to establish the value of the study of the past not as an end in itself, but as a way of providing perspectives on the present that contribute to the solution of problems peculiar to our own time.

—Hayden White, "Interpretation in History"

In "Interpretation in History," Hayden White suggests that interpretation enters historiography through the ethical and ideological choices made by historians, choices that affect the ways any given representation can be used for the comprehension not only of the past but also of current social problems (70). From this point of view, history is not just a study of the past as "an end in itself," but "a way of providing perspectives on the present that contribute to the solution of problems peculiar to our own time." I begin with this reference to White's work because his emphasis on the ethical dimensions of the interpretive choices made by historians is relevant to the leap I would like to make in this chapter from the past to the present, specifically in terms of the significance that histories of activist rhetorics hold for ongoing pedagogical work in the field of rhetoric and composition. I have left a discussion of historiography and its relationship to this project until the concluding chapter because doing so allows me to review the histories I have recounted in order to raise questions about how pedagogical history will affect rhetoric and composition curricula as more and more local and specific histories emerge within the field.

While it is true that the present is indeed always a new pedagogical and historical moment, it is imperative, as I have suggested throughout this book, that we recover the legacies of activist educators in other periods who foregrounded the politics of writing and speaking instruction in the courses they designed and taught. The voices of these remarkable teachers and students echo throughout the preceding chapters. Their struggles and achievements present a rich and complex portrait of activist education in practice at particular social and political moments. But their voices are only a few of the many voices of teachers and students that must be brought to our attention if we are to begin to sketch a portrait of the history of activist rhetoric education in the United States; we are only now beginning to recover many of the pedagogical artifacts of educators and their students who confronted language and learning issues that are not dissimilar to those that students, educators, and educational policy makers face today.

And yet the present moment is not identical to others in which particular forms of activist education emerged. How then, might we, as White suggests, make use of the educational histories of disparate periods? What might educators who sought to address issues of difference in the rhetoric classrooms of the past tell us about how we should go about that project? I explore these questions in more detail in this final chapter as well as suggest what it is that we might learn from the enactments of activist rhetoric courses of Jordan, Brown, Norton, Colby, and Budenz by placing the challenges and achievements of these educators and their students in the context of more recent debates.

Like the educators in this study who taught in moments that were influenced by the tenets of the progressive education movement, contemporary educators have great opportunities, due to the momentum inspired by the present emphasis on multiculturalism, to address many of the same kinds of curriculum deficiencies that were met in an activist fashion in turn-of-the-century America. While the term *multiculturalism* is itself contested on many fronts (an issue that I address later in the chapter through an investigation of borderlands theory), there can be no doubt that it has altered or at least seriously challenged the shape of curricula within and across disciplines in the 1990s.[1] I suggest that these and other changes are part of a third wave of activist education in the history of the twentieth-century

American university. The first wave of changes came in the early part of the century through the influence of the progressive education movement, and the second wave through '60s reforms that led to open admissions and community colleges generated by the political climate of the civil rights movement and the Vietnam era. In recent years we have witnessed a third wave of educational reforms most visible in attempts made within colleges and universities to acknowledge the increasingly diverse student population of the colleges and universities of the United States. This transformation, while affecting such different disciplines as science and history, continues to be particularly influential in English studies. Certainly the challenges to the Western canon have dramatically changed the nature of the field, for today students study writers whose names would never have appeared in the same courses fifteen years ago. The result is that numerous institutions have made significant strides in bringing a curriculum to the university that honors the histories, literatures, and linguistic traditions of a diverse student population.

Composition studies, like other disciplines, have been altered by this third wave of educational reform. New research challenges conceptions of rhetorical instruction as a "politically neutral" form of schooling. By focusing on the inherent political dimensions of the rhetoric classroom, educators now examine a number of issues that have begun to alter composition pedagogy in important but controversial ways. These developments include but are not limited to (1) classroom work that asks students to examine the relationship between language and identity, (2) assignments that are designed to help students investigate issues of difference and promote critical consciousness, and (3) courses that make a vital connection between rhetorical study and service.

One might ask, however, what is significant about these particular pedagogical emphases? How do these three categories relate to one another? As I argued in chapter 1, these features of rhetorical instruction emerge repeatedly in the history of our discipline and help to raise the following questions about rhetorical education: What or whose language do we value in the rhetoric classroom and what are the consequences of those linguistic choices? What issues are important enough to constitute a place in the rhetoric classroom? And to what ends should we and our students direct our rhetorical expertise?

These pedagogical emphases are significant, not only in terms of the questions they raise about the ethics of rhetorical instruction, but also in terms of what they mean in relation to one another. Implicit in them is a logical progression from an emphasis on the individual to an emphasis on the social or communal. Consider that an individual must know who he or she is in the world before he or she can position himself or herself in relation to larger social issues. Pursuing the relationship of language and identity through an analysis of discourse communities helps students to recognize that the relationship between words and self is indeed a powerful one. In addition, assignments that ask students to interrogate social issues that affect their lives teach students how to think critically—to question ideas and concepts they might have believed were beyond question. Without the development of critical consciousness, students cannot easily make the transition from the individual to the communal. Insofar as the study of the relationship between language and identity is concerned, the achievement of critical consciousness readies the student to take on a social identity, to determine what his or her response to particular issues should be. These three features are very much a part of contemporary pedagogical debates and, as I have argued throughout this book, part of a long history of activist rhetorical instruction in American colleges and universities.

What follows, then, is an attempt to connect past and present through an examination of contemporary manifestations of these features of activist rhetorical instruction and the controversy that surrounds them. I argue that the understanding of how educators addressed issues of difference in the rhetoric classroom in other times will help us to maintain the present momentum inspired by multiculturalism and allow us the opportunity to further interrogate issues of difference and to make them part of ongoing curricular reform in colleges and universities in the United States.

Race, Class, Gender, and the Contested Territory of Language and Identity

A variety of media events have placed the subject of language and identity front and center in a host of educational debates. Recent manifestations of this focus are evident in the controversy surrounding the barrage of recent books on gender and communication and in the conflicting views over Ebonics. Less obvious is the renewed emphasis on workers' education and its attentiveness to complex interrelations between communication and working-class identity. I wish to stress, however, that while debates over the relationship between language and identity have not always been carried out under the national scrutiny of an Ebonics controversy or public attention devoted to disputes over gendered communication, educators and students throughout the history of popular education have been forced to consider the connection between modes of communication and perceptions of self and community. I will trace here, briefly, some of the most important manifestations of these debates as they have played out in recent educational history to provide a more contemporary context for the issue. I will also reconsider the ways that Jordan, Brown, Colby, Norton, and Budenz addressed this issue in their courses and pedagogical materials.

Perhaps, though, I should first ask why the subject of language and identity continues to generate so much controversy in and out of the rhetoric classroom. It may be because, as Henry Giroux observes, language is so integral to the construction of self:

> It is through language that we come to consciousness and negotiate a sense of identity, since language does not merely reflect reality but plays an active role in constructing it. As language constructs meaning, it shapes our world, informs our identities, and provides the cultural codes for perceiving and classifying the world. (*Schooling and the Struggle* 46)

Giroux's understanding of the ways that language constructs a sense of identity is echoed by others who emphasize that the teaching of writing and speaking is controversial for the very reasons that Giroux describes—because the *word* is tied so directly to the *self.* Language conditions whatever sense of selfhood we possess and makes the contemplation of self possible.

But what if the language that conditions self is outlawed and denigrated? In *Pedagogy of the Oppressed,* Paulo Freire, like others who have taught in literacy programs designed to serve the disenfranchised, describes his understanding of the mediating power of language and the critical relationship between epistemology and the word: "Dialogue," he writes, "is the encounter between men, mediated by the world, in order to name the world. Hence, dialogue cannot occur between those who want to name the world and those who do not wish this naming—between those who deny others the right to speak their word . . ." (69). This mediating feature of language, as Freire makes clear, is a crucial aspect of the issue of language and identity, and it is the reason why students need to be taught to think reflectively about what language is, how it functions, and how communal modes of communication are negotiated and enforced.

During the 1960s, the teaching experiences of a number of educators led them to restructure writing instruction with a new attention to issues of difference during what has come to be called the "open admissions" era. Adrienne Rich, Mina Shaughnessy, and other teachers who were instrumental in this important phase of the City College of New York worked to create one of the first nationally visible campaigns to address a population of students in the composition classroom frequently ignored by educators and other institutions. In "Teaching Language in Open Admissions," Rich describes how she came to understand the potentially oppressive use of academic discourse in the lives of students and why she needed to think carefully about how she responded to their uses of "nonstandard" English:

> I think of myself as a teacher of language: that is, as someone for whom language has implied freedom, who is trying to aid others to free themselves through the written word, and above all through learning to write it for themselves. . . . I have always assumed, and still do assume, that people come into the freedom of language through reading, before writing; that the differences of tone, rhythm, vocabulary, intention, encountered over years of reading are, whatever else they may be, suggestive of many different possible modes of being. But my daily life as a teacher confronts me with young men and women who have had language and literature *used against* them, to keep them in their place, to mystify, to bully, to make them feel powerless. (63)

In this passage Rich articulates the sentiments of other writing teachers and composition theorists who later emphasized the pedagogical dilemmas surrounding language and identity in their work. Such sentiments grew out of and were confirmed by the now legendary resolution of the Executive Committee of the Conference on College Composition and Communication in 1974. "We affirm," the Executive Committee wrote,

> the students' right to their own patterns and varieties of language—the dialects of their nurture or whatever dialects in which they find their own identity and style. Language scholars long ago denied that the myth of a standard American dialect has any validity. The claim that any one dialect is unacceptable amounts to an attempt of one social group to exert its dominance over another. Such a claim leads to false advice for speakers and writers, and immoral advice for humans. A nation proud of its diverse heritage and its cultural and racial variety must have the experiences and training that will enable them to respect diversity and uphold the right of students to their own language. (2–3)

This document suggests a number of reforms and considerations for teachers of English at all levels, challenging them to understand that nonstandard varieties of English do not represent inferior thinking and that, as Mary Jordan knew, teachers of English need more knowledge of the history of the English language and its continual changes in vocabulary, syntax, and pronunciation.[2] Most important, the 1974 CCCC resolution (it has recently been reissued) emphasizes the cultural stakes for students who are placed in the position of having to abandon one variety of English for another. It recognizes that because "dialect is not separate from culture, but an intrinsic part of it, accepting a new dialect means accepting a new culture; reject-ing one's native dialect is to some extent a rejection of one's culture" (6). The overt articulation of the connection between language and culture in this passage and elsewhere in the document is striking, particularly its emphasis on what students gain and lose when they learn to speak stan-dard English.[3] In many ways this statement calls to mind one made by Mary Jordan in *Correct Writing and Speaking,* where she observes the conflict of the student who studies a "consistent form of English," and who is brought "into open rebellion against the idioms that he has used all his life and that are as dear to him as his home, his church, and his dead" (9).

But those who design curricula seldom have been interested in the cul-tural degradation imposed by what has been termed the "deficit model" of English writing and speaking instruction. Geneva Smitherman notes that in the 1960s, black students were introduced to language studies and remediation programs for the "disadvantaged" and "culturally deprived." Called "compensatory education" programs, these remedial pedagogical approaches often spoke of a cognitive-linguistic "deficiency" in black stu-dents. Conceived within an ideology of "black pathology," such programs ultimately treated African American English as an inferior discourse, and this had devastating results on the rhetorical education of African Ameri-cans (*Talkin'* 201–2). One of the disgraces of the deficit model of language instruction, according to Smitherman, was its suggestion that schools must compensate for a cultural deficiency in families. Her critique echoes that of Basil Bernstein, who explains that compensatory education "serves to di-rect attention away from the internal organization and the educational context of the school, and focus our attention upon the families and chil-dren . . ." (qtd. in Smitherman, *Talkin'* 203). In doing so, it identifies the African American linguistic realm as inferior or incorrect and alleviates the pedagogical responsibility of educators to teach writing and speaking in ways that do not dishonor the linguistic culture of African American students.

Some resistance to the deficit model of rhetorical instruction was mounted in 1979 when a federal district court reached a decision in favor of eleven African American children in Ann Arbor, Michigan, who, it was charged, were harmed by their teachers' attitudes about African American English. Although this decision concerned African American students at Martin Luther King Jr. Elementary School, it had national implications for the lan-guage and identity debate. The court held the Ann Arbor School District Board responsible for failing to teach children whose home language was African American English. By drawing on the testimony of experts in so-ciolinguistics and education to establish that "African American English is a rule-governed language system, and that the teachers' failure to recognize this linguistic fact led to negative attitudes toward the children who spoke it," attorneys in the case demonstrated that the educational progress of students was hindered by the failure of teachers to address the issue effectively (Ball and Lardner 472). This legal decision drew attention to the pedagogical and psychological damage inflicted by the deficiency model, and it marks a historical moment when pedagogical attitudes began to shift. However, in the nearly twenty years between the Ann Arbor decision and the Oakland Schools Ebonics resolution (1996), views of African American English have not changed sufficiently. The outrage expressed over these events is an example of educational racism that has proved to be a barrier to pedagogical reform.

Even so, that educators have drawn attention to writing and speaking pedagogies that dismiss the cultural heritage of others throughout history should not be a point lost on those who create social and educational policy. We must not fail to understand the important legacy of this issue, for its history shows us that it is an ethical issue—one that has been with us for some time. This is precisely Smitherman's point in a recent article that argues (more than twenty years after the publication of her landmark *Talkin' and Testifyin'*), that the debate over the relationship between language and identity will continue to haunt us until we address it adequately. Smitherman emphasizes that the issue of language and identity is one that needs more press and more discussion in educational circles where so many policies that affect students' lives are made. In "CCCC's Role in the Struggle for Language Rights," Smitherman recounts the long struggle for the Students' Right to Their Own Language declaration of the early seventies. While her work focuses primarily on African American vernacular, current debates have an even broader history than we have acknowledged and that history includes the struggle over class and regional issues of language use.

Educators have long witnessed the effects of unreflective rhetoric instruction on students who are culturally invested in "nonstandard" varieties of English. Certainly this is one of the reasons that the CCCC resolution takes up this issue. The document also resonates with many features of the earlier pedagogies of Jordan, Brown, Colby, Norton, and Budenz whose work with specific student constituencies made it impossible to ignore how the relationship between language and identity affects the teaching of writing and speaking. These educators understood that if they were to teach effectively, they would need to help their students gain a complex awareness of language and to honor language diversity in its various forms.

In the decades since Rich and Shaughnessy first wrote about teaching writing at City College and CCCC issued the resolution on Students' Right to Their Own Language, Shirley Brice Heath, Mike Rose, David Bartholomae, Anthony Petrosky, and others have begun to move writing teachers away from a "deficiency model" in terms of pedagogical theories that suggest how writing teachers might address issues of difference in the rhetoric classroom through attention to language and discourse communities. Although he does not address the issue of language and identity specifically, Bartholomae has been instrumental in articulating the challenges that face students who have historically had a difficult time succeeding in the university. He makes it clear that students are forced to learn a set of standards that are governed by a wide variety of contexts and conventions to which they are unaccustomed:

> Every time a student sits down to write for us, he has to invent the university for the occasion—invent the university, that is, or a branch of it, like History or Anthropology or Economics or English. He has to learn to speak our language, to speak as we do, to try on the peculiar ways of knowing, selecting, evaluating, reporting, concluding, and arguing that define the discourse of our community. Or perhaps I should say the *various* discourses of our community, since it is the nature of a liberal arts education that a student, after the first year or two, must learn to try on a variety of voices and interpretive schemes—to write, for example, as a literary critic one day and an experimental psychologist the next, to work within fields where the rules governing the presentation of examples or the developments of an argument are both distinct and, even to a professional, mysterious. ("Inventing the University" 273)

What makes Bartholomae's work particularly innovative is that it encourages an overt attention to the ways that language functions in different contexts; in this way his pedagogical orientation contributes to debates surrounding language and identity because he urges students to develop a heightened sense of modes of communication. Although Bartholomae has been much criticized for this particular essay by those who see his work as a call for excessive assimilation on the part of students, I would argue that his articulation of the obstacles facing students is quite a development in the history of composition studies. Since Shaughnessy first argued that there was a method to the "errors" of basic writing students, compositionists have turned their attention to new ways of understanding what it is that teachers can do to help students who have historically faced the greatest difficulties in learning to write in the university and to look for more complex

BORDERLANDS, INTERSECTIONS, AND ONGOING HISTORY

reasons why they have often failed in schools where a profound ignorance of and disrespect for the relationship between language and identity permeates the curriculum.

To understand how the issue of language and identity has become so prevalent in recent years, I want to explore manifestations of the debates inside and outside academic circles. Consider, for example, the enormous amount of attention devoted to the many books on gender, identity, and communication. Of the numerous scholars working in this area, Deborah Tannen's work is probably most widely known. In *You Just Don't Understand*, Tannen describes the gendered language practices in American culture and how they profoundly affect relationships in the home, school, and workplace where asymmetries in forms of communication often create a climate of misunderstanding. By foregrounding questions surrounding gender and language, researchers such as Tannen have done much to help educators and students to become aware of the biases of gendered linguistic conventions.

Despite the fact that Tannen's work has received a great deal of positive attention and has inspired debates about the nature of gendered communication practices and their effects in a wide variety of contexts, it has come under intense attack from those who wish to dismiss its claims and the subject of gendered communication altogether. In a scathing *New Republic* review of a number of Tannen's books, Alan Wolfe rejects Tannen's ideas in an essay titled "She Just Doesn't Understand." Suggesting that Tannen's work lacks "scientific evidence" and "normative argument," Wolfe's critique epitomizes many of those by others who trivialize research on this subject. Admitting his own biases against sociolinguistics (Tannen's field) and against ethnographic research (Tannen's method), Wolfe dismisses the relevance of her claims. Highly critical of Tannen's thesis that we need to better understand how gendered misunderstandings generate conflict and confusion, Wolfe takes her to task for what is, in his estimation, essentially an assault on democratic process. Because he believes that Tannen fails to celebrate good old-fashioned American dissent, Wolfe writes of her:

> This is not a voice of reason, equality and fair participation. This is a voice that, applied to the rough and tumble public world, delegitimates opposition and corrodes democratic practice. It is a good thing that there exists neither scientific evidence nor strong moral and normative argument to back it up. (35)

Such dismissals of theories that examine gendered communication practices miss what is really at stake in such debates. The canons of reason, equality, and fairness that Wolfe assumes to be available to all is precisely what is at issue, for he fails to understand how the "universal" qualities he describes are not disinterested. Indeed, Tannen's research challenges the kinds of values Wolfe assumes to be beyond question. Her work makes it clear that the attention we devote or deny to this subject will have far greater consequences than whether an author succeeds or fails to make an academic argument. For research on gender and communication has important implications for the lives of female students, particularly where education is concerned. Much of the current research on girl's schooling cites growing evidence indicating the dangers of educating girls and women in environments where no thought has been given to gendered communication practices and the relationship between them and learning. The work of Carol Gilligan, Peggy Orenstein, and Mary Pipher illustrates the ways in which girls are socialized to deny and subvert their goals, feelings, and behaviors in a manner that undermines their academic progress. Integral to the work of these researchers is an attention to language practices that instill particular patterns of communication in girls and women in a wide range of academic settings that can often be detrimental to learning and undermine the very possibility of "fairness."

Fortunately, educators in a number of fields are devoting increasing amounts of attention to the subject of gender and learning, and consequently to the subject of gender and communication. In terms of the writing classroom, feminists in the field of rhetoric and composition have done much to demonstrate the gendered nature of the rhetorical tradition and the impact of gendered pedagogies on students. Elizabeth Flynn, Susan Jarratt, Lynn Worsham, and many other theorists connect gender studies more directly to writing and speaking instruction, insisting that gender needs to be a central concern in composition research. As Jarratt makes clear in her introduction to *Feminism and Composition Studies,* this emphasis has changed the landscape of the field:

> Feminisms overlap composition studies, developing a growing body of work on discourses and practices of difference, representation, and the social construction of knowledge and its subjects; composition studies speaks to feminist inquiry where it investigates gendered differences in language, teaching, and learning—the very places where subjects take shape in writing, reading, and teaching contexts. . . . These, and many more touchpoints between feminisms and composition studies, suggest the rich possibilities located at their intersection. (3)

The forms of feminist inquiry that Jarratt describes make their presence felt in many kinds of scholarship, but the fact that feminist work on this topic has also appeared in a number of books and articles circulating outside an academic context suggests that this issue continues to receive a great deal of press largely because so many people recognize that there is a relationship between language and identity.

Controversial as they are, however, concerns about gender and communication practices are not without precedent. Mary Jordan, for example, demonstrated a similar awareness in the texts she generated on rhetorical theory as well as gender and learning. As a woman in a mostly male professoriate, Jordan could not ignore the effects of gender on the study of writing and speaking. We can see that her text challenges some of the received ideas promoted by her male contemporaries by means of its method of indirection and in terms of its focus on the history of the English language. In the early moments of her rhetoric text, Jordan provides a history of the English language to dislodge notions of an unchanging standard, notions that could potentially restrain women who studied rhetoric without the benefit of a traditional education, such as those who studied in women's clubs where Jordan's *Correct Writing and Speaking* text was frequently used. Her educational treatises speak more directly to the issue of gender and learning—an issue, as I have noted, that currently receives great attention recently in national educational debates. Jordan's educational treatises are important to the history of rhetoric because they call for separatist education in a time when many progressive feminists were calling for coeducation. Jordan advocated a rigorous course of study for her constituency of college women, one she believed to be superior to those of men's colleges. Her work suggests that she understood how important it was for women to pursue their educational goals in academic settings that would value their ideas as well as their modes of expressing them.

While issues of gender and communication have been very much in the public eye lately, language issues surrounding race have been no less public and no less controversial. Perhaps no other media event better represents the controversy over language, identity, and race than the fury over Ebonics. In 1996, the Oakland, California, school board voted to implement a new program giving Ebonics, or African American English, legitimate second language status in its schools with the assumption that this practice would help African American students to learn standard English. Much to the school board's surprise, a national debate erupted, and the events surrounding the decision became so inflamed that the district was eventually forced to drop all references to the word *Ebonics* and to implement the project by incorporating the ideas behind Ebonics without the controversial name.

What became an often misunderstood feature of the Ebonics debate had to do with the negative characterization of Ebonics as another language entirely, one that would be "taught" at the exclusion of "standard English" (Smitherman and Cunningham 228). Parents and educational policy makers of many races worried that teachers would teach African American English instead of standard English and that this pedagogical orientation would further ostracize an already disenfranchised student population. But those who understood Ebonics in this way were mistaken. For Ebonics was never intended to be taught in place of standard English. Rather, the strategy was that teachers would use Ebonics as a vehicle to other modes of communication and as a way to understand the value of different varieties of English in various contexts.

In "Moving Beyond Resistance: Ebonics and African American Youth," Geneva Smitherman and Sylvia Cunningham argue that the issue of language and identity must be addressed in curriculum design. They maintain that when black youth feel that they must make a choice between one variety of English and another, it becomes more likely that they may reject education altogether. Smitherman and Cunningham contend that students need to examine black English and standard English in light of one another, to explore the ideological forces that shape our understanding of different forms of communication. Without the development of this kind of linguistic awareness, African American students may reject standard English without ever consciously knowing why they do so or what the consequences of doing so will mean in their lives. "Many of our students," Smitherman and Cunningham write, "resort to not-learning as a means of resistance; a way to hold on to the one part of themselves that they feel cannot be taken away. Although we should encourage this stance, at the same time, we need to help them move beyond the resistance that keeps them stifled and saddled in the same place" (230).

Like the course of rhetorical study advocated by Bartholomae that asks students to recognize the changing language conventions of different contexts, proponents of Ebonics emphasize that students need to understand the ideological consequences of complex linguistic social negotiations. Such an awareness, they argue, will help students to demystify the dominant discourse before they unconsciously accept or reject it.

However, like the backlash against research on gendered discourse, the backlash against the Ebonics movement dismisses the relationship between language and identity and makes light of an issue that has serious educational and social consequences. Characteristic of many assaults on Ebonics is this one by John Leo who diminishes the complexity of the Ebonics debate by reducing it to the level of superficial politically correct school policy: Leo asserts that championing Ebonics means championing

> public tolerance for the politically correct notions lurking in the shadows of this debate—identity politics, victimization and self-esteem theory. Identity politics means a constant attempt to stress cultural separateness, so a claim to a separate language, rooted dubiously in "Niger-Congo" idioms," fits right in. To the PC-minded, what most of us call the mainstream is known as "the dominant culture," and the same overtones of oppression and bias are turning up in the Ebonics lobby: Standard English is "establishment" language or "standard" English (in quotes to show contempt). So any attempt to educate black children in ordinary English is a psychic assault and a sort of linguistic colonialism. (20)

Those who, like Leo, deny the psychological and social consequences of what he flippantly calls "linguistic colonialism" fail to see that in the absence of a purposeful investigation of the relationship between language and identity, many African Americans will, and do, drop out of school. Leo and many others who oppose Ebonics conflate this movement with bilingual education, and even though the evidence supports Leo by suggesting that Hispanic children outside the bilingual system learn English faster than those inside it, such comparisons are problematic in that, in one case, we are talking about a variety of English, and in the other case, another language altogether. To fuse the two educational issues in this way is misguided; for although African American English vernacular is often referred to as another language, it is really one of many varieties of English. This distinction, in the minds of many educators, particularly those who promote Ebonics, makes a good deal of difference.

Another oversight by many critics of Ebonics concerns their treatment of Ebonics merely as a pedagogical trend. Many assume, incorrectly, that Ebonics is a pedagogical orientation without historical precedent. They overlook the fact that the issue has arisen again and again for educators and students over time because of its relationship to educational ethics. Those who oppose Ebonics because they believe it to be a pedagogical trend would do well to examine the reemergence of the issue throughout history. African American scholars have long critiqued the disdain of those like Leo, who support racist pedagogical approaches to the teaching of writing and speaking. In *The Mis-Education of the Negro* (1933), Carter G. Woodson underscores the "pathology approach" that Smitherman argues is so often applied to African American English:

In the study of language in school pupils were made to scoff at the Negro dialect as some peculiar possession of the Negro which they should despise rather than directed to study the background of this language as a broken down (i.e., linguistically polluted by English) African tongue—in short to understand their own linguistic history, which is certainly more important for them than the study of French Phonetics or Historical Spanish Grammar. (qtd. in Smitherman, *Talkin'* 203)

In this passage Woodson articulates a need to approach the study of speaking and writing from a rhetorical point of view. That is to say, he observes the importance of study that goes beyond simply learning how to express oneself—a study that examines the history of rhetoric and the evolution of particular modes of communication and their ideological consequences.

Twenty years before the publication of Woodson's book, Hallie Quinn Brown fashioned an elocutionary curriculum for the African American community in the extracurricular materials she designed for her students. Given the important legacy of this issue, educators must become aware that other rhetoric teachers have, throughout history, refused to disparage a variety of English that has strong currency for some members of the African American community. Clearly, this is an understanding possessed by Brown, evidenced in the early-twentieth-century elocution materials she produced for African American students inside and outside the university. While her emphasis on standard English makes it clear that she recognized that such language conventions increased the potential for African Americans to progress in white society, Brown's text also features African American English to deliver the essence of an embodied rhetoric, and it indicates that she had some awareness of the important relationship between language and identity. Brown lived in a time when a black woman educator did not have the opportunity to articulate all of the social and political implications of language for the African American community of turn-of-the-century America. Even so, her work (like that of educators committed to Ebonics) embodies pedagogical features that stress the situated nature of the curriculum she promoted to recognize the cultural identity of African Americans in the post–Civil War era. It appears that Brown, as well as contemporary educators supporting the Ebonics movement, hoped to demystify standard English by emphasizing the nature of linguistic conventions so that students might feel freer to move between the languages of a wide variety of communities. When understood in this way, Ebonics is hardly the radical pedagogical proposition that it has been perceived to be in the media. It is, however, an example of the bitter debates that ensue when educators challenge the perceived neutrality of language instruction—the universal disinterestedness Wolfe articulates in relation to Tannen.

Examples of class-based communication are much less conspicuous and more problematic to discuss; there are, it seems, no recent events surrounding class identity and language that rival the media attention received by the Ebonics movement or the many books published recently on gender and communication. This lack may be due to the fact that class is a different kind of category from that of gender or race because the demarcations of class are less rigid and more permeable. It may also be due to the strong ideological position of asserting the irrelevance of class to social life in late-twentieth-century America. However, if we consider the literacy practices currently enacted by workers from a wide variety of backgrounds, we may gain some awareness of how a relationship between class and communication remains an important one, even in an era when class boundaries are much more difficult to identify. One recent phenomenon figures prominently in this respect: the revitalization of the workers' education movement. This educational movement is currently growing throughout the United States. Labor studies programs affiliated with major universities across the country are more and more plentiful, and unions are again sponsoring workers to study in these programs where the entire curriculum, particularly the rhetoric curriculum, is overtly politicized in terms of labor interests and, I would argue, class identity. For example, at the University of Minnesota, one of many labor studies programs founded to educate trade unionists in the country, course materials are written with this particular student constituency in mind. In *Labor Guide to Local Union Leadership*, Gene Daniels, Roberta Till-Retz, Lawrence Casey, and Tony DeAngelis outline a course of rhetorical study for those students who are learning to use their rhetorical expertise in the service of the unions. A survey of the table of contents in this text reveals the ideological nature of this particular pedagogy. Among the many chapters on facets of communication in the labor context are those on "Labor's Message Through the Media;" "Conducting Union and Committee Meetings;" and "Personal and Public Communication Techniques." While many portions of the book draw on traditional pedagogical models, all of the examples are contextualized in terms of the labor movement. Consider this example on the power of nonverbal communication:

> Nonverbal cues can even *substitute for* the verbal message if they are powerful and unambiguous enough, as when an emblem is displayed and words become unnecessary. Think, for example, of the most powerful scene in the movie *Norma Rae*—when the protagonist climbs on the table and slowly

rotates holding up her hand-made sign UNION so that all workers can see the physical demonstration of the idea of unity against the employer. Tears can substitute for words (and also make them impossible!), as when a beloved union leader says good-bye and retires. When the long-time head of the Minnesota AFL-CIO rose to give notice that the 1984 state convention would be his last, he could not continue because his tears spoke with more eloquence of his feelings about the labor movement than the words he had written. (314)

In a manual with hundreds of examples like this one, specifically contextualized in terms of labor union issues, this text, like many before it, demonstrates the importance of site-specific rhetorical education. Like the rhetoric courses at Brookwood in the twenties and thirties, these courses at Minnesota and other locations are designed to help labor worker activists consider language and its political manifestations in a wide variety of rhetorical situations. In an era where organized labor has a soiled reputation, the reemergence of labor education in this century represents an important return to the concerns of class identity and language.

However, scholarly investigations of the relationship between working-class identity and language vary from those that have been undertaken by researchers examining race and gender and their connection to linguistic identity. Unlike work on race, gender, and communication practices, those who work on language and class identity cannot easily identify features of a discourse that could be called "working-class vernacular." However, it seems that it is possible to talk about the relationship among class, language, and identity without identifying a working-class vernacular, but rather by identifying historically and culturally specific manifestations of language that are class-driven. Most of the research that has emerged on the issue of language and class identity comes out of sociology and labor history and focuses on the working-class history of Great Britain. It is worth referring to in this context, however, because such work represents attempts by researchers in other fields to examine the relationship between language and class consciousness. In light of poststructuralist theories of language, a number of labor historians and sociologists in the 1980s and 1990s began to consider how language works to mediate working-class experience and class consciousness. In *Languages of Class,* Gareth Stedman Jones argues that labor historians must confront language theory if they are to understand the context-bound notions of class and move beyond the limitations of social history that avoids linguistic analysis. Stedman Jones writes:

I became increasingly critical of the prevalent treatment of the "social" as something outside of, and logically—and often, though not necessarily, chronologically—prior to its articulation through language. . . . "class" is a word embedded in language and should thus be analysed in its linguistic context; and secondly, that because there are different languages of class, one should not proceed upon the assumption that "class" is an elementary counter of official social description. . . . (7)

If notions of class are bound by cultural and historical contexts, one way to observe the variations is by observing language in those various contexts. While no forms of communication remain static, if we are to study the ways in which language functions to create a sense of working-class consciousness and identity in twentieth-century America, we must be attentive to linguistic transformations. New sites of labor education in America represent contexts in which we might observe the ways that language functions to construct a sense of working-class identity in a specific cultural and historical moment.

These instances of pedagogical debate over language and issues of difference represent only a few of the ways that the relationship between language and identity continues to shape pedagogical discussions. They suggest that this controversy is not likely to disappear anytime soon. It is for this reason that these issues demand historical attention and a more intense commitment on the part of educators to understand the ways such issues have been addressed over time. While educators have not always addressed the subject of language and identity in the spotlight that illuminates this topic of late, some educators considered the embodied nature of communication practices in educational sites where they could not be ignored given the student constituencies they served.

Politics and Pedagogy: Multiculturalism and Critical Consciousness

Another significant feature of the activist rhetoric curricula that has endured over time is the emphasis educators have placed on the study of rhetoric and civic responsibility, or, in more contemporary terms, on rhetoric and social action. In the following section I discuss this issue, but here I raise the subject of critical consciousness and the assignments that make such thinking possible. This feature of rhetorical instruction is in fact one that has been emphasized throughout history; it is a tradition that dates to classical times.

An important distinction exists, however, between the elitist rhetorical tradition in classical times and the writing and speaking courses that form the basis of the activist rhetorics I am studying. The opportunity to study rhetoric in classical Greece was permitted only by a small privileged portion of the population, excluding women, slaves, and others outside an elite social class. It was against the entrenched elitism of this long tradition that many of the educators I name here designed alternative rhetoric courses, courses overtly politicized in terms of the interests of specific student constituencies, constituencies that throughout history have been ignored by many academic institutions.

And yet despite the differences between the elitism of the classical tradition and the activist rhetorics engineered by the educators in this study, the long-standing connection between rhetorical study and civic responsibility or social action must be acknowledged. Such a connection demonstrates the political power of language to inspire action on the part of citizens, to articulate responses to civic and social problems. Many educators and administrators in the past and present have considered courses in writing and speaking to be politically neutral courses. As increasing numbers of scholars work to address the myth of language neutrality, thus emphasizing the ideological aspects of writing and speaking instruction, it has become obvious that how we teach, the language conventions we teach, and the themes we discuss and write about in the classroom are ideological and connected to issues in the larger culture. Many of the current educational debates over the politics of writing instruction have occurred in response to efforts by educators to underscore the relationship between the study of rhetoric and civic action. By asking students to write about controversial issues such as racism, sexism, and economic exploitation, educators have challenged the perceived neutrality of the rhetoric classroom even as they have emphasized the age-old relationship between the study of rhetoric and civic debate.

The suggestion by many scholars that language instruction, as well as writing and speaking instruction, has political effects has generated controversy, a controversy that has long been tied to the rhetoric classroom (Bullock and Trimbur; Bizzell). In revisiting the subjects of recent educational debates about the rhetoric course, I argue here that such controversies are not new; rather, they have been the driving force of the rhetoric curriculum since the study of rhetoric originated in ancient Greece.

One incident that is indicative of what is at stake in current debates over the curriculum of first-year writing courses and their relationship to civic debates occurred at the University of Texas a decade ago. Attempts to adopt a new curriculum for English 306 in 1990 precipitated national media attention to the politics of writing instruction. When Linda Brodkey, head of the Lower-Division English Policy Committee, revamped the freshman writing course known as E 306 and called it "Writing about Difference," a curricular war broke out inside and outside the University of Texas. A departmental curriculum committee decided to give the course a one-year trial run, and the committee approved the use of Paula S. Rothenberg's book *Racism and Sexism*. The book was selected because of its use nationwide in writing courses on race and gender issues. All instructors scheduled to teach the course were to attend an orientation on how to conduct classes that included discussions about social differences. After the approval of both the course and the text, a number of faculty members who lost a department vote on the course took their objections to the press. Alan Gribben, a professor in the English department, was primarily responsible for leading a media crusade to have the new version of the course canceled. The consideration of issues such as race and gender in the composition classroom, he and many of his colleagues argued, had nothing to do with the writing curriculum. What could placing controversial topics at the center of such a course do to help students learn to write? Indeed, the course materials were believed to be so radical that *Texas Monthly* ran a story about how "literary terrorists" were plotting to overthrow the UT Department of English and indoctrinate the students.

Over a period of months, the incidents at UT incited such controversy and conversations about the events were carried out at such a national level, including forums such as morning talk shows and the *New York Times*, that two weeks before the first day of classes the new version of the course was canceled and teachers were left without a syllabus or text. The pressure placed on the president of the university from alumni and those outside the university eventually resulted in his cancellation of the new course. In the wake of this controversy, however, educators everywhere were given a new occasion to contemplate the politics of writing instruction (Faigley 74–75).

I mention this incident because the resistance mobilized against English 306 at the University of Texas is representative of the kind of national hostility that has developed in response to proposed curricular changes in writing courses associated with multiculturalism. Such resistance is widespread. Moreover, it is hypocritical, it seems, in light of the long precedent of aligning civic issues with rhetorical training. Why call for courses that do not reflect an attention to the political nature of language? To do so is to establish courses that are not connected in important ways to the lives of students and events in the larger culture outside the university; ignoring the politics of writing instruction means designing courses that do not provide opportunities for students to consider language in the rigorous tradition of rhetorical study that dates to classical times.

We might ask, however, for a more detailed sense of what that rigorous rhetorical tradition entailed in classical times and throughout history. What, for example, were the manifestations of the tradition of classical rhetoric in the European university? In what forms did classical rhetoric emerge in the American university in the nineteenth and early twentieth centuries? And, if considerations of civic issues and the preparation for civic participation have, throughout history, often been an integral component of the rhetoric course, when and how did such considerations disappear from the rhetoric curriculum of the American university?

We would do well to remember that to speak of rhetoric is to speak of a 2,500-year-old discipline—one that has been transformed over time. It is, however, a discipline that has always taken as its primary purpose the study of persuasion. Robert Connors explains that rhetoric originated in the probate courts of early Syracuse, and the forms of rhetorical practice generated there taught students how "to create persuasive arguments, to develop and win cases, to put forward opinions in legislative form, to stake out turf and verbally hold it against opponents in public contest" (25). Students were trained to examine a wide variety of civic issues and to debate them, because these were skills they would need outside the academy. Because of this practical but important feature of rhetorical training, rhetoric was at the center of the curriculum. The supposition that controversial issues had no place in the rhetoric classroom would have appeared ludicrous to students and teachers during classical times because a consideration of such issues was at the very heart of rhetorical study. There would have been no reason to study classical rhetoric were it not for the assumption that it was preparation for civic participation.

Given the long history of this agonistic emphasis in the classical rhetoric curriculum, it is puzzling how the focus on public discourse could disappear as the major emphasis in rhetoric courses in the American University. However, as a number of scholars point out, the long precedent of rhetorical study for civic training was dramatically altered in the United States during the nineteenth and early twentieth centuries. While debate, with all its agonistic flair, flourished outside the academy, within academic institutions of higher education in the United States the emphasis on rhetorical training was transformed in a number of important ways. According to Connors:

> The shifts in rhetorical ideas and teaching were rapid and extraordinary, and they proceeded on several levels. There was the shift from oral rhetoric to a rhetoric of writing. There was a shift from theoretical to practical rhetoric. There was a shift from argumentative rhetoric to multimodal rhetoric. The very culture of rhetoric, which had always informed Western education, turned from a public, civic orientation meant to prepare leaders of church and state toward a more privatized, interiorized, and even artistic orienta-

tion meant to aid in self-development or career preparation in bureaucratic organization. (23)

Such changes mark a significant development in the history of rhetoric because, interestingly, the change from "a public, civic orientation to a more privatized, interiorized, and even artistic orientation" signals, in many ways, the opening of institutions and the study of rhetoric to others who had not typically been given the opportunity to study its principles in academic settings. Certainly, it opened rhetorical study to those who prepared for professions other than the law, politics, or clergy. I would argue, however, that this shift is also due to restraints in the larger culture that kept "others" from participating in the democratic processes of the United States during this time. In other words, it was not believed that everyone who studied rhetoric in nineteenth-century America needed it to participate in the political realm of the nation, since so many inhabitants of the United States at this time were not believed to be citizens in any genuine sense of the word.

I would point out that in the sites pertinent to this study, the pedagogy of the rhetoric classroom appears to have been built very much on a rhetoric of citizenship—through an emphasis on debate and contest. For if mobilization for any form of political activity could be perceived as preparation for citizenship, then the activist rhetorics of Jordan, Brown, Colby, Norton, and Budenz can be viewed in the tradition of rhetorical training for civic participation.

Consider, for example, the assignments generated by Jordan for her Smith students. Such assignments, as I have illustrated, were clearly politicized in terms of women's issues of the particular time. Although women did not have the vote throughout much of Jordan's teaching career, and while Jordan opposed suffrage herself, she gave the women in her courses opportunities to contemplate a wide variety of issues relevant to the politics of their location, such as the nature of women's education, suffrage, and the responsibilities of educated women to their less educated sisters. From Jordan's educational treatises and from her textbook we have discerned why she believed it was so important for women to have the opportunity to pursue a rigorous education apart from men. While students in Jordan's courses read Aristotle, Plato, Carlyle, and other texts that routinely comprised courses of rhetorical study in men's colleges, the assignments Jordan generated were sharply politicized in the interests of women. Through them she offered her students a forum to contemplate their own position in the culture and to determine what their own politics should be.

Likewise, African American students of Brown were provided with opportunities to consider and critique the racism of turn-of-the-century

America. The readings presented in Brown's reciter text gave African American students of elocution knowledge of African American history and urged them to consider how they might help to improve conditions for blacks in post–Civil War America. Although the readings in her reciter text are not actual assignments that call for students to write or speak extemporaneously on topics concerning the politics of their location, the fact that Brown includes selections on African American history such as the Battle of Port Hudson, where black forces helped defeat the Confederacy, or slave narratives that describe the horrors of slavery, indicate the nature of the politicized elocution curriculum she offered in *Bits and Odds*. It was here that those who practiced reading her selections would encounter important historical events that were not preserved or celebrated in mainstream reciter texts—moments in African American history that were not easily obtained or valued in other forums. That so many of Brown's selections examine the accomplishments of and abuses to African Americans is a significant feature of the politicized nature of her materials.

Perhaps more so than Jordan and Brown—Colby, Norton, and Budenz offered an overt course of politicized rhetorical study to their students. Their efforts were clearly focused on preparing labor activists to make gains, through their rhetorical expertise, for the exploited worker of various industries. In requiring students to write employment autobiographies and deliver speeches designed to convert others to the labor movement through an examination of low wages and dangerous working conditions, rhetoric teachers at Brookwood had clearly and intentionally asked students to contemplate the politics of their location in such assignments. Their rhetoric curricula addressed many of the central issues important to these student constituencies, and the assignments they presented to their students were offered as a means of urging them to think and write about issues that may have been ignored or treated peripherally at more traditional academic institutions.

I raise the issue of contest and debate, of citizenship, of groups of people with different interests, because the work of the activist educators I focus on here extended their work beyond the academy to engage women, African Americans, and members of the working class as citizens. The emphasis on multiculturalism has, in many ways, helped to return rhetorical education to the civic focus that has been so much a part of the discipline since classical times. While the rhetorical tradition, as it existed then, could not be said to have included women, underrepresented ethnic groups, or members of the lower classes—the very groups that multiculturalism seeks to address and represent—the curricular emphasis on issues of citizenship formed the basis of the course of rhetorical study. It is this feature of classical rhetoric that has revitalized contemporary rhetoric studies: Edward Corbett, Patricia Bizzell, Ira Shor, and many others have done much to reconceptualize first-year writing courses on a broad scale in terms of a rhetoric that takes up civic issues as a central concern. When Corbett's *Classical Rhetoric for the Modern Student* first appeared in 1965, it was one of the first texts in the second half of the twentieth century to challenge educators to establish rhetoric and composition courses that turned students' attention to political topics as they studied writing and rhetoric. Corbett's newly generated context for many of the important features of classical rhetoric did not so much revise the classical tradition as extend it to better serve the needs of a student population situated in a particular historical moment. As increasing numbers of educators looked to revitalize classical rhetoric and the civic connection that had always been so much a part of rhetorical study, their efforts increasingly recognized a concern for disenfranchised students; thus, they sought to enact writing courses that could help these students explore social issues most connected to the politics of their location. It has only been in recent years that these changes in the composition curriculum have been greeted by an audience of educators and educational policy makers who view the inclusion of controversial topics in the composition curriculum as a radical proposition. Such a position denies the fact that controversial issues have always stood at the center of the classical rhetoric curriculum for much of the 2,500 years since its inception in ancient Greece. It demonstrates a refusal to see that such issues change over time depending on specific historical and cultural circumstances. Those educators who were instrumental in helping to bring down the controversial version of English 306 at the University of Texas would have done well to reflect on this long-standing feature of rhetorical training before canceling a course designed to help students debate issues of difference that matter beyond the technicality of language—subject matter that demands the discourse of contest in a society that has lately turned a good deal of its attention to such matters.

Service-Learning and the Composition Classroom

In addition to specifically foregrounding the politics of writing and speaking instruction through attention to language, identity, and curricula that investigate social problems, compositionists have begun to critique what many inside and outside academic institutions see as the isolationist project of higher education by raising questions about what the relationship between the university and the larger culture ought to be. For much of American history, colleges and universities outlined in their mission statements the shaping of moral character of undergraduates as one of the goals of higher education. However, as schools became more secularized, an overt articulation of these aims became less common. Recently, educators and students have returned to the question of how similar objectives might be addressed in secularized colleges and universities. As a recent article on service-learning in the *New York Times* points out,

> In a time of outward tension and inner searching, when many Americans worry about social decay and also show a growing interest in spirituality, students, teachers, and administrators on campuses are asking whether colleges ought to try once again to build moral and spiritual character as well as intellect. . . . a number of colleges and universities are devising ways to try to give greater weight to issues of personal ethics and community responsibility—whether by writing new mission statements, hiring staff to promote such discussions or encouraging students to think of social service projects in terms of moral or religious responsibility. (23–24)

Although service-learning is a phenomenon occurring within many different disciplines, it is currently a major focus of numerous composition programs in colleges and universities throughout the country. In academic institutions such as Stanford and Carnegie Mellon, students examine the ways writing functions in social service contexts as they examine their own relationships through writing to those in the larger culture. In service-learning courses, students are regarded as a kind of worker-scholar. They work in environments outside the classroom in ways that augment the classroom experience and provide opportunities for them to question how education might do more than increase one's economic status.

Implementing the ideals of service-learning courses, however, is a decidedly controversial and complex endeavor because questions about social structures, ideology, and social justice are not automatically raised in classes that emphasize a community service component. Neither are they as easily answered as Wolfe suggests earlier in his intonation of equality, reason, and fairness. These abstract categories of equality, reason, and fairness raise questions about the level, for instance, on which these categories are to be measured. They are precisely the site of the contests mentioned in the last section. Even when such issues are foregrounded, students find it difficult to move beyond socialized conceptions of individualism and the Horatio Alger myth that anyone can "transcend" any social problem. Because it is likely that many students, given their socialization, will focus on the individual instead of the larger social structure, they may miss the important distinction between personal catastrophe and social injustice. According to Bruce Herzberg:

> If our students regard social problems as chiefly or only personal, then they will not search beyond the person for a systemic explanation. Why is homelessness a problem? Because, they answer, so many people are homeless. The economy is bad and these individuals lost their jobs. Why are so many people undereducated or illiterate? Because they didn't study in school, just like so-and-so in my fifth grade class and he dropped out. (309)

Herzberg's efforts to combat the myth of American individualism manifested themselves in his own section of a service-learning composition course that made the study of literacy and schooling a primary focus of the class. He assigned students *Lives on the Boundary* by Mike Rose, *Savage Inequalities* by Jonathan Kozol, and selections from *Perspectives on Literacy,* an anthology edited by Kintgen, Kroll, and Rose. In this two-semester course, students studied literacy theories and issues and wrote about them for the first semester. In the second semester, they used their literacy training to begin tutoring at a local homeless shelter, working with residents to write resumes and job application letters. While Herzberg explains that students did demonstrate compassion for the residents and worked well with them, he saw how formidable the obstacles were to helping them to transcend the myth of American individualism. The goal of his course was not to offer students tutoring experience but to investigate the social and cultural reasons for the existence of illiteracy and to better understand why their efforts were needed so much in this context.

Courses like Herzberg's are taught now in numerous institutions. Although service-learning, as I suggested earlier, is indeed a phenomenon that has manifested itself in many different disciplines, we might ask why much of it is taking place within composition studies and to what ends. Some might argue that the goal of composition courses is to teach students solely how to write, not how to reflect on social problems such as hunger, homelessness, and illiteracy. And yet, as I have argued, civic issues have historically been part of the rhetoric curriculum; since classical times, the study of rhetoric has been embedded with an examination of the political issues that are most crucial to society at any given moment. Asking students to think and write about these issues while they are in direct contact with people affected by social problems makes sense; it emphasizes the relationship between *civic consideration* and *civic action.*

I have already argued that civic considerations were an important component of the activist rhetorics I describe in this study. However, I would also suggest that the insistence on the part of these educators to consider controversial issues that were relevant for these student constituencies resulted from their awareness of the important relationship between the issues they asked students to think and write about and the social actions they hoped students would perform. Jordan, Brown, Colby, Norton, and Budenz integrated the goal of service with other important pedagogical features of their rhetoric curricula. They encouraged students, and said as much in the pedagogical materials they generated, to use their rhetorical expertise in ways that would be beneficial to other women, African Americans, and members of the working class.

Consider Mary Jordan, for example, whose rhetoric curriculum reminded her students of the privileges afforded to them because they received a college education in a time when most women did not have this opportunity. Like Brown, Colby, Norton, and Budenz, Jordan emphasized that the price of educational privilege was service. She reminded women in her courses that they should not forget their less advantaged sisters, who worked in factories without the economic benefits afforded to the students of Smith who, by and large, came from an elite social class. In addition, Jordan hoped that her students would do more, after leaving Smith, to increase educational opportunities for women. Among the more politicized assignments she gave in her rhetoric courses was one that asked students to write a convincing argument for the merits of higher education for women with an audience in mind that did not support such educational endeavors at the time.

Hallie Quinn Brown also emphasized the feature of service within her elocutionary course of study. Imploring those students who studied elocution from her texts to consider their obligation "to the man who is down," Brown consistently argued in her pedagogical materials and educational treatises that education without a dedication to service was a vain and selfish proposition. She urged her readers to use their education, not for personal financial gain, but in the service of others, for the person in "the delta, canebrake, cotton field, and rice swamp." This feature of Brown's elocutionary pedagogy is very much absent from the curricula generated by other elocutionary theorists who did not write and work from her position as a black woman in a society founded on white supremacy. In contrast to these pedagogues, Brown's educational philosophy was very much embedded with the now legendary "Lifting as We Climb" motto of the National Association of Colored Women, an association for which Brown served as president in 1924.

In a fashion similar to those of Jordan and of Brown, Colby, Norton, and Budenz also emphasized the relationship between rhetoric and service. Only students who established a previous record of service to the labor movement were admitted to Brookwood. Stressing the principles of service within the curricula they proposed, Colby, Norton, and Budenz built assignments into the curriculum that routinely asked students to consider the misfortunes of others and what solutions they might offer to ease the malaise experienced by so many others affected by poor wages and dangerous working conditions in various industries across the nation.

Rethinking Pedagogical History: Activist Rhetorics in the Borderlands

The contemporary pedagogical issues I trace in this chapter have their roots in earlier historical and cultural moments. Even so, these issues and events, in both their contemporary and historical manifestations, indicate a discipline that is now and has in the past been engaged by the relationship between language and identity; schooling and critical consciousness; and education and service. I do not imply that these issues were never considered at all in more traditional colleges and universities in the United States; I simply argue here that these pedagogical features figured prominently in the rhetoric courses taught by these educators and were designed to address the needs of specific student constituencies. How, then, can we learn from them, situated as we are in another time, in academic institutions that have increasingly complex student demographics? In keeping with the spirit of the epigraph that opens this chapter, I suggest that there are connections we can make between the pedagogies of these varying historical moments. I argue as well that considering contemporary rhetorical theory and pedagogical history can be useful to educators who wish to redefine methods of implementing the tenets of multiculturalism in the rhetoric classroom.

But to speak of multiculturalism is to speak of a term that is contested on many educational fronts. I want to suggest, as many proponents of multiculturalism have, that in its most simple and basic terms, multiculturalism be theorized in a more complex manner. I turn to the work of Borderlands theorists to support my efforts in this endeavor, in order to examine the identity politics that have become so much a part of the American school curriculum in the nineties and to suggest how Borderlands theory might help us to understand and transform the activist rhetorics I have described for our time. I think this theory can be useful in demystifying the deceptively homogeneous communities of students to which the educators in my historical study addressed themselves, for the student constituencies for whom Jordan, Brown, Colby, Norton, and Budenz designed activist rhetoric curricula were more complex than they may appear. They were more than communities comprised of women, African Americans, and members of the working class. To view issues of difference such as gender, race, or class issues separately—in isolation from others—is problematic for the reasons Gloria Anzaldúa and other Borderlands theorists describe. Anzaldúa writes, "The borderlands are physically present wherever two or more cultures edge each other, where people of different races occupy the same territory, where under, lower, middle and upper classes touch, where the space between two individuals shrinks with intimacy" (qtd. in Read 111). The borderlands are places that invite a more sophisticated interrogation of difference and challenge identity politics by providing attention to a multiplicity of voices.

While other theories of difference have made an important contribution to the evolution of progressive politics in American education, they have also been flawed and reductionistic. In many ways, Borderlands theory grows from the discourse of radical feminists who have complicated feminist theory and the wide array of differences between women of varying ethnicities, classes, and sexual orientations that challenge the myth of a unified feminism. In a similar manner, Borderlands theory challenges narrow conceptions of multiculturalism and "political correctness" that pose a serious threat to ongoing dialogues surrounding education and issues of difference. For useful as such theories have been, they contribute to essentialist practices that ultimately endanger the dialogue. Giroux speaks to the ways that Borderlands theory can complicate traditional discussions of multiculturalism and its implications for educational reform:

> The concept of border pedagogy suggests not simply opening diverse cultural histories and spaces to students, but also understanding how fragile identity is as it moves into borderlands crisscrossed with a variety of languages, experiences, and voices. There are no unified subjects here, only students whose voices and experiences intermingle with the weight of particular histories that will not fit into the master narrative of a monolithic culture. . . . This is not a call to romanticize such voices. It is instead a suggestion that educators construct pedagogical practices in which the ideologies that inform student experiences be both heard and interrogated. (*Border Crossings* 174–75)

When issues of identity are complicated in the way Giroux suggests, we can begin to understand that creating and implementing curricula that respond to the needs of a diverse student population will never be a simple prospect. Certainly the work of the educators in this study demonstrates this fact. For as extraordinary as these modes of rhetorical instruction generated for women, African Americans, and members of the working class proved to be, we must see that these pedagogies were not easily or effortlessly enacted, particularly in a society that was generally opposed to the higher education of these groups of people. Clearly, Jordan, Brown, Colby, Norton, and Budenz struggled to help disenfranchised students achieve rhetorical expertise and political agency under remarkable conditions. In many ways, their experiences show that the enactment of critical education is an infinitely more complex endeavor than theories of critical pedagogy theorists have acknowledged. It is our work to complicate the efforts of these dedicated and effective teachers. Because students and teachers in these particular academic communities defined themselves beyond the limiting constructs of race, class, or gender, numerous issues surrounding identity intervened in the process of critical education in ways that have only recently begun to be discussed in terms of "border pedagogy."

While theorists are beginning to address how the complexity and diversity of "Other" shapes critical education, there have been few contemporary accounts of actual classroom practice and even fewer historical accounts that explore how the permeable and sometimes contradictory categories of difference affect critical education. The individual complexities of those who participated in rhetorical education at Smith, Wilberforce, and Brookwood emphasize the dynamic interplay of factors that shape rhetorical instruction in any site. Exploring these dynamics in historical terms has been one intention of this project, for, despite the apparent homogeneity of these student constituencies, the academic communities at these institutions, as well as those outside them (for many pedagogical materials were aimed at the citizen outside the university), were not unified.

In the case of Mary Jordan, for example, students opposed their teacher when she disagreed with them on the question of suffrage. Jordan believed, unlike many of her students and colleagues, that women could work effectively for women's issues outside the political venues that historically had been established and controlled by men. Jordan's own views and their presence in the rhetoric classroom help to demonstrate how competing "feminisms" operated in late-nineteenth- and early-twentieth-century culture and within the classrooms of women's colleges where women debated the future of their role in the society at large. Viewing Jordan's position in relation to that of many of her students—especially now in relation to our history—helps to illustrate how complex activist education can be in a community where students do not see the nature of their problems or the manner in which they should be addressed in the same way.

Similar contradictions may be seen to exist in the pedagogical orientation of Hallie Quinn Brown. The message Brown articulated as an elocutionist to her black audience must have appeared contradictory at times, for although she advocated elocution as a practice that could lead to social consciousness in the lives of African Americans, her position in regard to language practices may have appeared elitist to those without the most basic literacy skills. From a late-twentieth-century perspective, this tension in her work is apparent, particularly in an age when Audre Lorde has proclaimed that "the master's tools will never dismantle the master's house" (112). Lorde argues that no genuine change can come from the use of a language that cannot represent the linguistic reality of oppressed people. Even so, Brown's conviction that literacy could be used to help the disenfranchised groups resonates with Mary Louise Pratt's understanding of the "transcultural" efforts by which marginalized people adapt materials transmitted to them by a dominant culture to be used for their own ends. Certainly through her performances and lectures, Brown adopted particular linguistic practices for specific contexts. While she appears to have advocated the master's language, she also preserved black English and folklore through her performances. As she worked to give other African Americans the same educational opportunities that she had, Brown generated numerous scholarships for prospective Wilberforce students and extended the influence of Wilberforce University through her many lectures and elocutionary tours as she educated African Americans about their history, folklore, and language.

In a similar fashion, Josephine Colby, Helen Norton, and Louis Budenz negotiated comparable tensions at Brookwood Labor College. They faced animosity from the unions who accused them of communist tendencies, as well as criticism from students who sometimes saw their teachers not as labor leaders but as "radical" academics out of touch with the problems of labor activists. Of the three institutions, Brookwood possessed the most overt policy on student involvement in adopting curricula, awarding scholarships, and voting on the hiring of new teachers. Such endeavors, it seems, we can see in retrospect, were conducted very much in a Freirian spirit. Yet in 1924, the school's director, A. J. Muste, reveals that the power bestowed on students was largely a superficial gesture. While many of the school's major decisions were made by a group comprised of six faculty members and thirty-seven students called "The Brookwood Cooperators," Muste points out discrepancies in the policy, noting that

> students have exercised only advisory power in most important educational and administrative matters, and the faculty, for example, has generally strenuously opposed the granting of further power under the present scheme.

Regardless of whether the students should or should not have further power under this or any other scheme, the fact that in theory they have one thing but in practice a very different thing under the present arrangement, has undoubtedly been a cause for both confusion and irritation.

The involvement of students in the process of hiring and curriculum development was almost unheard of in other institutions. While Brookwood faculty members could not ultimately eradicate the power dynamics between students and teachers, that they attempted to devise a process by which students could participate in the educational vision of the institution was a rather bold undertaking indeed. Even so, Muste's document indicates that this effort was not easily or perhaps ever enacted, and it gives us some sense of the nature of the challenges faced by the academic community of Brookwood.

These instances demonstrate just a few of the conflicts and contradictions that emerged through attempts to establish curricula for specific student constituencies that are apparent because of the intersection of our contemporary work and their historical experience. This complicated history asks us to redefine what we mean when we say pedagogy is successful or unsuccessful and whether such judgments are "fair." Certainly it is difficult to judge the success of the activist rhetorics of these contexts if we define the success of the curriculum by the activism of the students. While we know that many Brookwood students went on to become influential labor activists, little is known about the students of Jordan or Brown. We can only speculate about the kinds of opportunities that were offered to nontraditional students, what those opportunities may have meant to them, and what they made of them. We must recognize, though, that an activist pedagogy does not in and of itself ensure political action. As Giroux points out, critical literacy does not equate itself with freedom but with the dialogue that makes freedom possible. "To be literate," he says, is *not* to be free: it is to be present and active in the struggle for reclaiming one's voice, history, and future" (Schooling 155). Certainly just as illiteracy does not explain the causes of massive unemployment, bureaucracy, or many other social problems, critical literacy neither automatically reveals nor guarantees social, political, or economic freedom. However, without critical literacy, marginalized people cannot participate in a dialogue that allows them to work for change through collective action.[4]

I avoid making assumptions about what the long-term effects of the pedagogies were or might have been partly because the kind of history I am advocating does not end or, as White says, is not an end in itself. I think we can speculate, however, that the opportunities provided to these students were important ones—that they offered students the chance to encounter rhetorical education that was designed with women, African Americans, and members of the working class in mind. I would also emphasize the fact that these educators and their students struggled as many of us struggle now to find ways of addressing difference in the classroom.

For there are clear challenges that present themselves when students are asked to examine the civic issues, particularly as they relate to issues of multiculturalism and difference, in the writing classroom. The crucial theoretical problem that arises when educators talk about difference is the dangers that exist in simply reinscribing a "melting pot" view of difference. While borderlands theory complicates identity politics, it also poses new challenges for educators. The danger is that educators and students alike may fail to see how crucial it is to examine the cultural differences that affect language and other cultural practices and that they may ignore the pedagogical attention these issues demand in the classroom.

Gary Olson offers an excellent critique of multiculturalism as it has been enacted frequently in composition courses. Connecting the multicultural movement to ethics, Olson argues that though postmodern critiques of traditional ethics make sense, many theorists now take issue with the postmodern idea that no system of ethics can reliably regulate human behavior. Ethics, Olson emphasizes, takes on more importance in the postmodern age: "far from being dead, ethics is perhaps more alive than ever, for now we must *actively participate* in our own moral decision making, no longer abdicating our responsibility to external forces" (46). He believes that ethics has been reconceived through an encounter with others in a wide variety of courses and curricula. While underscoring that the multicultural move in composition studies is an important one, Olson perceives the very real difficulties the opportunity to encounter and interrogate "Other" poses for compositionists who seek to implement this sort of pedagogical emphasis. Such pedagogy is problematic when it is deployed as a kind of liberal pluralism, or what Joseph Harris calls a "'multicultural bazaar,' where students 'are not so much brought into conflict with opposing views as placed in a kind of harmless connection with a series of exotic others'" (qtd. in Olson 47).

Olson suggests that postcolonial theory can reinvigorate and illuminate many of the pedagogical problems and possibilities that exist when educators attempt to implement a curriculum that examines the intersections of discourse, ideology, and community. By implementing writing courses that ask students to examine the nature of the medium of language, how language functions to create particular kinds of power dynamics, ideologies, and strategies to effectively harness such knowledge in the community, students can investigate issues of difference and the role that language plays in constructing those dynamics.

In the current educational climate, pedagogies for the rhetoric classroom that acknowledge the challenges of confronting difference are desperately needed. As teachers, politicians, and other educational strategists in the United States continue to wage a struggle over educational policy for a diverse nation, at stake are both curricular and pedagogical models designed to address particular kinds of educational goals. The debate thus far has centered largely on the extent to which a country as diverse as the United States can claim a "national culture." Many educational conservatives, such as E. D. Hirsch and Dinesh D'Souza, for example, view the United States as a meritocracy in which all students have the same opportunity for success because they all have the opportunity to receive education. Because many conservative educators see educational sites as locations to foster national and civic pride, as well as a unified notion of culture, they have advocated educational reforms that ignore difference on the basis of the threat it poses to a national unity. Among their proposed solutions to the current educational controversies have been the National Standards Curriculum and the English Only movement, which seek to cultivate a cultural literacy through texts that have "universal" meanings that transcend various social and cultural groups within the United States.

While many educators oppose such efforts, few of them have turned to history to make a case for curricula that have historically sought to value issues of difference in the classroom. Few have attempted to reclaim detailed past enactments of liberatory pedagogy so that educational reform might be better understood through historical accounts. There is a need to recover accounts of activist education in practice, for without the voices of the teachers and students who participated in this kind of schooling at various historical moments, there can be no understanding of the ways in which pedagogy has evolved to meet the needs of a society composed of individuals of various backgrounds. Those scholars who examine the pedagogical history have yet to do much of the kind of "thick description," to appropriate the anthropological term of Clifford Geertz, that would produce a more specific understanding of the ways educators have dealt with issues of difference in the rhetoric classrooms of the past.

I have argued throughout this book that the curriculum recovery of activist educators such as Jordan, Brown, Colby, Norton, and Budenz and many others can and will help us as we chart courses for rhetorical education of the future. Those of us committed to making the university a place that honors the increasingly diverse student population of the country can aid that work by engaging in the kind of historical projects that White advocates when he calls on us to "establish the value of the study of the past not as an end in itself, but as a way of providing perspectives on the present that contribute to the solution of problems peculiar to our own time." While we must be aware that solutions of other moments may not—in fact, probably cannot—correspond or translate directly to our own context, we should not avoid such examinations, as some might argue, because it is impossible to apply the lessons they might have to teach to the present moment. I argue that the pedagogical questions for which we seek answers are not so much academic as they are ethical and social; they are forms of engagement that ongoing history pursues. In the present moment, the emphasis that many of us place on the issues of language and identity, the investigation of social problems in the writing classroom, and the integration of the study of rhetoric and service was often an emphasis of activist educators in the past. If we are convinced that such a mission should remain part of our endeavors, we need history to do that work better and more effectively.

John Dewey writes that "Every generation has to accomplish democracy over again for itself," that, in effect, it must be reinvented again by those who encounter new problems and new challenges to its ideals. He adds that democracy "is something that cannot be handed on from one person or one generation to another, but has to be worked out in terms of needs, problems and conditions of the social life of which, as the years go by, we are a part" (87). As we work to reconceive rhetoric studies in the new century, we must rely on the history of our discipline to inform our collective pedagogical imagination. Our students depend on us for curricula that will offer them a pedagogy of possibility—one that will help them understand their relationship to language as well as the implications that rhetorical study has for citizenship and service in their lives. To offer students this opportunity we need to engage, in our own ongoing history, the work of our pedagogical predecessors. For this reason—as well as for the inspiration they supply—their efforts are worthy of our study, adaptation, and application.

Notes

Works Cited

Index

Notes

1. Educational Politics: Rhetorical Instruction and the Disenfranchised Student

1. See Stephen Jay Gould's *The Mismeasure of Man* for a history of the methods used by a variety of physicians to argue for the biological inferiority of African Americans, Native Americans, and working-class people. Among the methods examined by Gould are craniology, body measurement, and early IQ tests.

2. See Catherine Hobbs's introduction to *Nineteenth-Century Women Learn to Write* for a detailed overview of the history of women's literacy rates in early America through the nineteenth century. Hobbs examines cultural characterizations of women's literacy practices in a variety of contexts as well as attitudes and events that shaped rhetorical education over time.

3. Lynn Gordon observes in *Gender and Higher Education in the Progressive Era* that a number of women's rights advocates enlisted their efforts to refute Dr. Clarke's theories. According to Gordon:

> The *Woman's Journal,* the leading women's rights publication, printed highly critical reviews of Clarke's book by distinguished doctors and nonmedical authorities. Three volumes of essays, edited by suffragists Julia Ward Howe, Eliza Duffey, and Anna Brackett proclaimed Clarke's ignorance about women's health and education. College women were certainly conscious of the women's rights movement, if only because critics of women's higher education linked the two causes. (19)

4. Debates over the preferential course of study for African Americans were of course controversial in the African American community as well. The contrasting ideological positions of Booker T. Washington and W. E. B. DuBois over vocational versus academic institutions exemplify the split in educational vision for the race at this time. While DuBois supported professional education and Washington favored trade, the apparent dichotomy between them was more finely nuanced, according to Sterling Stuckey, who explains in *Slave Culture* that DuBois's critique of Washington was slow in coming because the two men shared the perception that "Economic power must underlie all efforts of the American Negro to establish himself." Although DuBois initially supported Washington in the 1890s, believ-

ing him to be a man of "high ideals," his critique of Washington came to fruition in *The Souls of Black Folk* and in his writings thereafter (S. Stuckey 269–73).

5. The Workers' Education Movement has a long history in the United States. For impressive histories of the movement, see Joyce Kornbluh's *A New Deal for Workers' Education* and Richard Altenbaugh's *Education for Struggle*. For essays on the history of the movement as well as on contemporary manifestations of workers' education in the United States, see *The Re-education of the American Working Class,* edited by Steven London, Elvira Tarr, and Joseph Wilson.

6. See Robin Varnum's *Fencing with Words* for an account of the rhetoric curriculum at Amherst College from 1938 to 1966. The course of study at this institution, though designed for a student population that was white, male, and from an elite social class is one example of how varied rhetoric instruction proved to be at different colleges and universities. Baird's legendary English 1-2 offered students intensive writing practice through the assignments that asked them to consider many philosophical and epistemological principles governing language practices.

7. See Condit and Lucaites' "The Rhetoric of Equality and the Expatriation of African-Americans, 1776–1826" for more on the racism and assumptions of the founding documents of the United States.

8. For a history of Wilberforce University, see Frederick McGinnis's *A History and Interpretation of Wilberforce University.*

9. For a history of Brookwood Labor College, see Charles Howlett's *Brookwood Labor College and the Struggle for Peace and Social Justice in America.*

10. See Joseph Kett's *The Pursuit of Knowledge under Difficulties* and Anne Ruggles Gere's *Intimate Practices: Literacy and Cultural Work in U.S. Women's Clubs, 1880–1920,* for impressive histories of rhetorical study and practice outside the formal academy.

2. Gender and Rhetorical Study: The Pedagogical Legacy of Mary Augusta Jordan

1. There is no indication that Jordan included or excluded women of color in her educational treatises. However, because she taught mostly white, economically privileged women, I have chosen to mark the term *women* as *white women* throughout this chapter.

2. For a very short time Jordan was engaged to her cousin, David Starr Jordan, who later became president of Stanford University.

3. Many educational feminists enlisted their energies in the battle for coeducation because they felt it was a more radical and ultimately more desirable goal. Rosalind Rosenberg observes that by 1872, there were ninety-seven colleges and universities in the United States that accepted women, though these institutions varied widely in educational quality and purpose.

4. For a detailed account of women and higher education in the United States during the nineteenth and twentieth centuries, see John Mack Faragher and Flo-

rence Howe's *Women and Higher Education in American History* and Mabel New-comer's *A Century of Higher Education for American Women.*

5. See Theodora Penny Martin's *The Sound of Our Own Voices: Women's Study Clubs, 1860–1910* and Anne Ruggles Gere's *Intimate Practices* for an overview of rhetorical study and critical literacy in women's clubs.

6. James Berlin provides an excellent overview of the Literacy Crisis at Harvard in the late nineteenth century. He explains that in 1894, the Harvard Board of Overseers became incensed at the errors it found in student essays, profoundly shocked that the best students in the country attending the best university in the nation had so much difficulty writing. "Rather than conclude that perhaps it was expecting too much of these students and their preparatory schools, however, the Board of Overseers excoriated the teachers who had prepared these students and demanded that something be done" (*Rhetoric and Reality* 24). Because secondary schools were blamed for the lack of preparation on the part of these students, "the Committee members focused on the most obvious features of the essays they read, the errors in spelling, grammar, usage, and even handwriting. They thus gave support to the view that has haunted writing classes ever since: learning to write is learning matters of superficial correctness" (61). The committee championed a composing process adhering to strict grammatical rules that became the emphasis of two of the most influential textbook writers of the late nineteenth century—Adams Sherman Hill and Barrett Wendell (*Writing Instruction* 61–62).

7. See T. R. Lounsbury's *History of the English Language* and *The Standard of Pronunciation in English.*

8. For a history of women who attended colleges and universities in the United States during the Progressive Era, from 1890 to 1920, see Lynn Gordon's *Gender and Higher Education in the Progressive Era.* Gordon examines the campus cultures (at the University of California; the University of Chicago; Yale University; Wellesley and Vassar Colleges) established by women of the period and the ways they linked the college curriculum to an extracurriculum of activism outside the university.

9. Mitchell was a neurologist specializing in women's disorders. He was Charlotte Perkins Gilman's psychiatrist and the object of criticism in her 1892 short story "The Yellow Wallpaper" (Ricks 66).

3. Elocution and African American Culture: The Pedagogy of Hallie Quinn Brown

1. For a detailed overview of the mainstream elocutionary movement, see Nan Johnson, "The Popularization of Nineteenth-Century Rhetoric: Elocution and the Private Learner" in *Oratorical Culture in Nineteenth-Century America,* edited by Gregory Clark and S. Michael Halloran.

2. See Charles Harris Wesley's *The History of the National Association of Colored Women's Clubs: A Legacy of Service* and Elizabeth Lindsay Davis's *Lifting as They*

Climb for impressive histories of the NACW and Hallie Quinn Brown's role within the organization. Anne Ruggles Gere also examines the history of the black women's club movement in *Intimate Practices: Literacy and Cultural Work in U.S. Women's Clubs, 1880–1920.*

3. Many of these women were present in 1893 at the World's Congress of Representative Women. Brown was one of six black women to address the delegates at the Columbian Exposition in Chicago. As Hazel Carby observes, "The struggle of black women to achieve adequate representation had been continually undermined by a pernicious and persistent racism and the World's Congress was no exception" (3–4).

4. Hazel Carby urges us to remember that the women who were most visible members of the NACW

> were not isolated figures of intellectual genius; they were shaped by and helped to shape a wider movement of Afro-American women. This is not to claim that they were representative of all black women; they and their counterparts formed an educated, intellectual elite, but an elite that tried to develop a cultural and historical perspective that was organic to the wider condition of black womanhood. (115)

5. See Shirley Wilson Logan's *"We Are Coming": The Persuasive Discourse of Nineteenth-Century Black Women* for a sophisticated analysis of the public persuasive discourse of nineteenth-century black women intellectuals. Logan examines the oratory of Maria Stewart, Frances Harper, Ida Wells, Fannie Barrier Williams, Anna Julia Cooper, and Victoria Earle Matthews as she identifies the important rhetorical strategies they used to make their messages heard in the United States during the nineteenth century. See Jacqueline Jones Royster's "To Call a Thing by Its True Name: The Rhetoric of Ida B. Wells" for an analysis of Wells's writing and oratory.

6. For a critical examination of Hurston's use of African American English vernacular, see Mary Helen Washington's "Zora Neale Hurston: A Woman Half in Shadow," in *I Love Myself When I Am Laughing . . . And Then Again When I Am Looking Mean and Impressive,* edited by Alice Walker (7–24).

4. Ideology and Rhetorical Instruction: Brookwood Labor College

1. For a detailed history of the events that inspired labor education, see Irving Bernstein's *The Lean Years: A History of the American Worker, 1920–1933.* Bernstein notes that the historic Red Scare resulted in the Palmer Raids of 1919–1920, which were an attempt by the government to ensure that a similar revolution did not occur in the United States. There was no labor legislation enacted during this period that would have helped organized labor make any significant gains. "Yellow-dog contracts" permitted employers to fire or refuse employment to anyone affiliated with a union. By the twenties, the AFL had become so debilitated that magazines and

newspapers routinely joked about the crippled organization. Union membership fell from 5 million in 1920 to 3.6 million in 1923 as fewer workers proved sympathetic to the message of organized labor (119).

2. A conference on workers' education was held in New York City on April 2, 1921, to discuss how industrial workers might be served by schools that aspired to meet their needs. A Workers' Education Bureau formed, and James Mauer, one of the founders and supporters of Brookwood became chairman of the organization. At the conference, participants discussed pedagogies, texts, characteristics of students and teachers, and the goals of an educational process designed to serve those who worked in industry. It was also during this time that organized labor offered its support to the workers' education movement. Although the American Federation of Labor would eventually accuse labor colleges of radical politics and withdraw financial support for them, this organization initially supported Brookwood and other labor colleges in their early days (Altenbaugh 38–39).

3. Some schools, as Berlin observes in *Rhetoric and Reality*, began to reconceive rhetoric curricula in terms of a social agenda by the time of the Depression. Such courses reinvented certain forms of rhetorical study in terms of writing about social problems but avoided a study of vernacular language that was believed to have no purpose in the larger culture.

4. See Lawrence Cremin for a history of the debate over the issue of language and culture that raged at this time. Numerous books and articles emerged in an era of controversy that rivals one we have witnessed more recently in the work of E. D. Hirsch and the late Allan Bloom. See, for example, *And Madly Teach* by Mortimer Smith and *Crisis in Education: A Challenge to American Complacency* by Bernard Iddings Bell.

5. See Len De Caux's *Labor Radical: From the Wobblies to the CIO.*

5. Borderlands, Intersections, and Ongoing History: Rhetoric and Activism in Higher Education

1. A number of critics have observed that much of the work on diversity and multicultural concerns risks avoiding the real work of interrogating difference in the academy by maintaining a superficial and vague consideration of what it means to be "Other." As Deepika Bahri argues,

> While it is not entirely clear what is meant by the term "culturally diverse," the diversity invoked is usually suggestive of some position of inferiority, marginality, or lack of access to resources more readily available to the mainstream. . . . The naming of the margin in euphemistic terms is a way of reducing discomfort and diverting attention away from precisely those problems of marginality, otherness and of historical particulars that should be addressed. (37)

2. While many historical documents use the term *dialect,* I consider *varieties of English* more appropriate in the present context.

3. Many of the articles that appear in *College Composition and Communication* during this period speak to the issue of language and identity in a much more radical tone than that which appears in most composition scholarship in the nineties.

4. See Shirley Brice Heath's *Ways with Words* and J. Elspeth Stuckey's *The Violence of Literacy* for an extended discussion of the relationship between literacy and social benefits and rewards.

Works Cited

Addams, Jane. "The College Woman and the Family Claim." *Jane Addams on Education*. New York: Teachers College P, 1985. 64–73.

Altenbaugh, Richard J. *Education for Struggle: The American Labor Colleges of the 1920's and 1930's*. Philadelphia: Temple UP, 1990.

Anzaldúa, Gloria. *Borderlands: La Frontera*. San Francisco: Aunt Lute, 1987.

Bahri, Deepika. "Terms of Engagement: Postcolonialism, Transnationalism, and Composition Studies." *JAC: A Journal of Composition Theory* 18.1 (1998): 29–44.

Ball, Arnetha, and Ted Lardner. "Dispositions Toward Language: Teacher Constructs of Knowledge and the Ann Arbor Black English Case." *College Composition and Communication* 48 (1997): 469–85.

Bartholomae, David. "Inventing the University." *Perspectives on Literacy*. Ed. Eugene Kintgen et al. Carbondale: Southern Illinois UP, 1988. 273–85.

Bartholomae, David, and Anthony Petrosky. *Facts, Artifacts, and Counterfacts: Theory and Method for a Reading and Writing Course*. Portsmouth: Boynton, 1986.

Bell, Alexander Melville. *The Principles of Elocution*. Salem: Burbank, 1878.

Bell, Alexander Melville, and David Charles Bell. *Bell's Standard Elocutionist*. New York: Funk, 1892.

Bell, Bernard Iddings. *Crisis in Education: A Challenge to American Complacency*. New York: Whittlesey, 1949.

Berlin, James. *Rhetoric and Reality: Writing Instruction in American Colleges, 1900–1985*. Carbondale: Southern Illinois UP, 1987.

———. *Writing Instruction in Nineteenth-Century American Colleges*. Carbondale: Southern Illinois UP, 1984.

Bernstein, Irving. *The Lean Years: A History of the American Worker, 1920–1933*. Boston: Houghton, 1960.

Bizzell, Patricia. *Academic Discourse and Critical Consciousness*. Pittsburgh: U of Pittsburgh P, 1992.

Bloom, Allan. *The Closing of the American Mind*. New York: Simon, 1987.

Bloom, Jonathan D. "Brookwood Labor College." *The Re-Education of the American Working Class*. Ed. Steven London, Elvira Tarr, and Joseph Wilson. New York: Greenwood, 1990. 71–83.

Brereton, John, ed. *The Origins of Composition Studies in the American College, 1895–1925*. Pittsburgh: U of Pittsburgh P, 1995.

Brophy, John. *A Miner's Life*. Madison: U of Wisconsin P, 1964.

Brown, Gillian. *Domestic Individualism: Imagining Self in Nineteenth-Century America*. Berkeley: U of California P, 1990.

Brown, Hallie Quinn. *Bits and Odds: A Choice Selection of Recitations for School, Lyceum and Parlor Entertainments*. Xenia: Chew, [c. 1910].

———. *Elocution and Physical Culture: Training for Students, Teachers, Readers, Public Speakers*. Wilberforce: Homewood, [c. 1910].

———. "First Lessons in Public Speaking." Appendix D. McFarlin. 156–172.

———. "Not Gifts but Opportunity." Appendix C. McFarlin. 173–181.

Buck, Gertrude. "Recent Tendencies in the Teaching of English Composition." *The Origins of Composition Studies in the American College, 1875–1925: A Documentary History*. Ed. John C. Brereton. Pittsburgh: U of Pittsburgh P, 1995. 241–51.

Bullock, Richard, and John Trimbur, eds. *The Politics of Writing Instruction, Postsecondary*. Portsmouth: Heinemann, 1991.

Campbell, JoAnn. "Controlling Voices: The Legacy of English A at Radcliffe College 1883–1917." *College Composition and Communication* 43 (1992): 472–85.

Carby, Hazel. *Reconstructing Womanhood: The Emergence of the Afro-American Woman Novelist*. New York: Oxford UP, 1987.

Clark, Gregory, and S. Michael Halloran, eds. *Oratorical Culture in Nineteenth-Century America: Transformations in the Theory and Practice of Rhetoric*. Carbondale: Southern Illinois UP, 1993.

Clark, Mary. Course essay. 1892. Smith College Archives, Northampton.

Colby, Josephine. Course materials. Box 5, Folder 4. Brookwood Labor College Collection. Archives of Labor and Urban Affairs, Wayne State U, Detroit.

———. Letter to Florence Rood. Box 27, Folder 3. Brookwood Labor College Collection. Archives of Labor and Urban Affairs, Wayne State U, Detroit.

Condit, Celeste Michelle, and John Louis Lucaites. "The Rhetoric of Equality and the Expatriation of African-Americans, 1776–1826." *Communication Studies* 42 (Spring 1991): 1–21.

Conference on College Composition and Communication. *The National Language Policy*. Urbana: NCTE, 1991.

———. *Students' Right to Their Own Language*. Spec. issue of *College Composition and Communication* 25 (1974).

Connors, Robert. *Composition-Rhetoric: Backgrounds, Theory, and Pedagogy*. Pittsburgh: U of Pittsburgh P, 1997.

Conway, Kathryn M. "Woman Suffrage and the History of Rhetoric at the Seven Sisters Colleges, 1865–1919." Lunsford 203–26.

Corbett, Edward P. J. *Classical Rhetoric for the Modern Student*. New York: Oxford UP, 1965.

Coulter, John. *The New Century Perfect Speaker*. Chicago: n.p., [1901].

Cremin, Lawrence. *The Transformation of the School: Progressivism in American Education, 1876–1957*. New York: Vintage, 1964.

Curry, S. S. *Foundations of Expression*. Boston: Expression, 1907.

Daniels, Gene, et al. *Labor Guide to Local Union Leadership*. Englewood Cliffs: Prentice, 1986.

Davis, Elizabeth Lindsay. *Lifting as They Climb*. New York: Hall, 1996.

De Caux, Len. *Labor Radical: From the Wobblies to the CIO*. Boston: Beacon, 1970.

Delsarte System of Oratory. New York: Werner, 1893.

Dennis, Peggy. *The Autobiography of an American Communist*. Berkeley: Hill, 1977.

Dewey, John. *Democracy and Education*. New York: Macmillan, 1916.

———. "Democracy and Education in the World of Today." *John Dewey The Later Works, 1925–1953*. Vol. 13. Ed. Jo Ann Boydston. Carbondale: Southern Illinois UP, 1988.

Dick, James M. "Problems of the Organizer." Box 1, Folder 3. Brookwood Labor College Collection. Archives of Labor and Urban Affairs, Wayne State U, Detroit.

Dimmock, George. "Mary Augusta Jordan." December 1979. Box 1, Folder 1. Sophia Smith Collection. Smith College Archives, Northampton.

Donaworth, Jane. "Textbooks for New Audiences: Women's Revisions of Rhetorical Theory at the Turn of the Century." *Listening to Their Voices: The Rhetorical Activities of Historical Women*. Ed. Molly Wertheimer. Columbia: U of South Carolina P, 1997. 337–56.

D'Souza, Dinesh. *The End of Racism*. New York: Free, 1995.

DuBois, W. E. B. *The Souls of Black Folk*. New York: Grammercy, 1994.

Elam, Diane. *Feminism and Deconstruction*. New York: Routledge, 1994. 105–20.

Faigley, Lester. *Fragments of Rationality: Postmodernity and the Subject of Composition*. Pittsburgh: U of Pittsburgh P, 1992.

Faragher, John Mack, and Florence Howe, eds. *Women and Higher Education in American History*. New York: Norton, 1988.

Farrell, Thomas J. "IQ and Standard English." *College Composition and Communication* 34 (1983): 470–84.

Fenno, Frank H. *The Peerless Speaker*. Chicago: Thompson, 1900.

Fisher, Vivian Njeri. "Brown, Hallie Quinn." *African American Women*. Ed. Dorthy C. Salem. New York: Garland, 1993.

Foner, Eric, and John Garraty, eds. *The Reader's Companion to American History*. Boston: Houghton, 1991.

Freeman, Lawrence D. "*The Students' Right to Their Own Language*: Its Legal Basis." *College Composition and Communication* 26 (1975): 25–29.

Freire, Paulo. *Education for Critical Consciousness*. New York: Seabury, 1973.

———. *Pedagogy of the Oppressed*. New York: Seabury, 1973.

Gates, Henry Louis. *The Signifying Monkey: A Theory of Afro-American Literary Criticism*. New York: Oxford UP, 1988.

Genung, John Franklin. *The Practical Elements of Rhetoric*. Boston: Ginn, 1886.

Gere, Anne Ruggles. *Intimate Practices: Literacy and Cultural Work in U.S. Women's Clubs, 1880–1920.* Chicago: U of Illinois P, 1997.

Gilligan, Carol. *In a Different Voice.* Cambridge: Harvard UP, 1982.

Giroux, Henry. *Border Crossings: Cultural Workers and the Politics of Education.* New York: Routledge, 1992.

———. *Schooling and the Struggle for Public Life: Critical Pedagogy in the Modern Age.* Minneapolis: U of Minnesota P, 1988.

Gordon, Lynn D. *Gender and Higher Education in the Progressive Era.* New Haven: Yale UP, 1990.

Gould, Stephen Jay. *The Mismeasure of Man.* New York: Norton, 1981.

Graff, Gerald. *Professing Literature: An Institutional History.* Chicago: U of Chicago P, 1987.

Handsome, Marius. *World Workers' Educational Movements: Their Social Significance.* New York: AMS, 1968.

Haraway, Donna. *Simians, Cyborgs, and Women: The Reinvention of Nature.* New York: Routledge, 1991.

Heath, Shirley Brice. *Ways with Words: Language, Life, and Work in Communities and Classrooms.* New York: Cambridge UP, 1983.

Hentoff, Nat. *Peace Agitator: The Story of A. J. Muste.* New York: Macmillan, 1963.

Hernstein, Richard J., and Charles Murray. *The Bell Curve: Intelligence and Class Structure in American Life.* New York: Free, 1994.

Herzberg, Bruce. "Community Service and Critical Teaching." *College Composition and Communication* 45 (1994): 307–19.

Hill, Adams Sherman. *The Principles of Rhetoric.* New York: American Book, 1895.

Hirsch, E. D. *Cultural Literacy.* New York: Vintage, 1988.

Hobbs, Catherine, ed. *Nineteenth-Century Women Learn to Write.* Charlottesville: UP of Virginia, 1995.

Hollis, Karyn. "Liberating Voices: Autobiographical Writing at the Bryn Mawr Summer School for Women Workers, 1921–1938." *College Composition and Communication* 44 (1994): 29–57.

Howlett, Charles F. *Brookwood Labor College and the Struggle for Peace and Social Justice in America.* Lewiston: Mellen, 1993.

Jarratt, Susan C., and Lynn Worsham, eds. *Feminism and Composition Studies: In Other Words.* New York: MLA, 1998.

Johnson, Nan. *Nineteenth-Century Rhetoric in North America.* Carbondale: Southern Illinois UP, 1991.

———. "The Popularization of Nineteenth-Century Rhetoric: Elocution and the Private Learner." *Oratorical Culture in Nineteenth-Century America: Transformations in Theory and Practice of Rhetoric.* Ed. Gregory Clark and S. Michael Halloran. Carbondale: Southern Illinois UP, 1993.

Jones, Gareth Stedman. *Languages of Class.* New York: Cambridge UP, 1983.

Jordan, Mary Augusta. "The College for Women." *Atlantic Monthly* Oct. 1892.

———. *Correct Writing and Speaking.* New York: Barnes, 1904.

———. "Higher Education." Association of Intercollegiate Alumnae. October 30, 1886. Box 3, Folder 98. Smith College Archives, Northampton.

———. "Noblesse Oblige." Pamphlet No. 36 of the Massachusetts Association Opposed to the Further Extension of Suffrage to Women." 1901. Box 3, Folder 104. Smith College Archives, Northampton.

———. "The Teaching of English in Smith College from Professor Seelye to President and Professor Neilson." June 1925. Box 3, Folder 111. Smith College Archives, Northampton.

Joseph Ozanic Collection. West Virginia U, Morgantown.

Kates, Susan. "The Embodied Rhetoric of Hallie Quinn Brown." *College English* 59.1 (1997): 59–71.

———. "Subversive Feminism: The Politics of Correctness in Mary Augusta Jordan's *Correct Writing and Speaking* (1904)." *College Composition and Communication* 48 (December 1997): 501–17.

Kett, Joseph. *The Pursuit of Knowledge under Difficulties: From Self-Improvement to Adult Education in America, 1750–1990.* Stanford: Stanford UP, 1994.

Kintgen, Eugene, Barry Kroll, and Mike Rose, eds. *Perspectives on Literacy.* Carbondale: Southern Illinois UP, 1988.

Kitzhaber, Albert. *Rhetoric in American Colleges, 1850–1900.* Dallas: Southern Methodist UP, 1990.

Kornbluh, Joyce. *A New Deal for Workers' Education: The Workers' Service Program, 1933–1942.* Urbana: U of Illinois P, 1987.

Kozol, Jonathan. *Savage Inequalities.* New York: Crown, 1991.

Kuhlman G., and A. Pierce. Memorandum. Box 96, Folder 6. Brookwood Labor College Collection. Archives of Labor and Urban Affairs, Wayne State U, Detroit.

Leo, John. "Ebonics? No thonics!" *U.S. News and World Report* 20 Jan. 1997: 20.

Logan, Shirley Wilson. *"We Are Coming": The Persuasive Discourse of Nineteenth-Century Black Women.* Carbondale: Southern Illinois UP, 1999.

London, Steven, Elvira Tarr, and Joseph Wilson, eds. *The Re-education of the American Working Class.* New York: Greenwood, 1990.

Lorde, Audre. *Sister Outsider: Essays and Speeches by Audre Lorde.* Trumansburg: Crossing, 1984.

Lounsbury, T. R. *History of the English Language.* New York: Holt, 1897.

———. *The Standard of Pronunciation in English.* New York: Harper, 1904.

Lunsford, Andrea A., ed. *Reclaiming Rhetorica: Women in the Rhetorical Tradition.* Pittsburgh: U of Pittsburgh P, 1995.

Martin, Theodora Penny. *The Sound of Our Own Voices: Women's Study Clubs, 1860–1910.* Boston: Beacon, 1987.

Marx, Karl. *The Eighteenth Brumaire of Louis Bonaparte.* New York: International, 1994.

McFarlin, Annjenette Sophie. "Hallie Quinn Brown: Black Woman Elocutionist." Diss. Washington State U, 1975.

McGinnis, Frederick. *A History and an Interpretation of Wilberforce University*. Wilberforce: Brown, 1941.

McLuhan, Marshall. *Understanding Media*. New York: McGraw, 1964.

Mohanty, Chandra Talpade. "On Race and Voice: Challenges for Liberal Education in the 1990's." *Between Borders: Pedagogy and the Politics of Cultural Studies*. Ed. Henry Giroux and Peter McLaren. New York: Routledge, 1994. 145–66.

Muste, A. J. "Memorandum in Re-Organization of Brookwood." Box 12, Folder 4. Brookwood Labor College Collection. Archives of Labor and Urban Affairs, Wayne State U, Detroit.

Myers, Constance Ashton. *The Prophet's Army: Trotskyists in America, 1928–1941*. Westport: Greenwood, 1977.

Newcomer, Mabel. *A Century of Higher Education for American Women*. New York: Harper, 1959.

Niebuhr, Gustav. "Colleges Setting Moral Compasses." *New York Times* 4 Aug. 1996, sec. 4: 23+.

Norton, Helen. Correspondence. Box 44, Folder 12. Brookwood Labor College Collection. Archives of Labor and Urban Affairs, Wayne State U, Detroit.

———. "Shop Papers". Box 4, Folder 12. Brookwood Labor College Collection. Archives of Labor and Urban Affairs, Wayne State U, Detroit.

Official Circular: Smith College. Northampton: Smith College, 1887.

Ohmann, Richard. *English in America: A Radical View of the Profession*. New York: Oxford UP, 1995.

Olson, Gary. "Encountering the Other: Postcolonial Theory and Composition Scholarship." *JAC: A Journal of Composition Theory* 18.1 (1998): 45–55.

Orenstein, Peggy. *Schoolgirls*: Young Women, Self-esteem, and the Confidence Gap. New York: Doubleday, 1994.

Pesotta, Rose. *Bread upon the Waters*. New York: Dodd, 1944.

Phelan, Craig. *William Green: Biography of a Labor Leader*. Albany: State U of New York P, 1989.

Pipher, Mary. *Reviving Ophelia: Saving the Selves of Adolescent Girls*. New York: Ballantine, 1994.

Pratt, Mary Louise. "Arts of the Contact Zone." *Profession* 91 (1991): 33–40.

Questionnaire for Prospective Brookwood Students. Box 12, Folder 21. Brookwood Labor College Collection. Archives of Labor and Urban Affairs, Wayne State U, Detroit.

Read, Daphnae. "Writing Trauma, History, Story: The Class(room) as Borderland." *JAC: A Journal of Composition Theory*. 18.1 (1998): 29–44.

Report on Brookwood Activities. Box 12, Folder 22. Brookwood Labor College Collection. Archives of Labor and Urban Affairs, Wayne State U, Detroit.

Rich, Adrienne. *On Lies, Secrets, and Silence: Selected Prose 1966–1978*. New York: Norton, 1979.

Ricks, Vickie. "In an Atmosphere of Peril." Hobbs 59–83.

Rose, Mike. *Lives on the Boundary: The Struggles and Achievements of America's Underprepared*. New York: Free, 1989.

Rosenberg, Rosalind. "The Limits of Access: The History of Coeducation in America." Faragher and Howe 107–29.

Royster, Jacqueline Jones. "'To Call a Thing by Its True Name': The Rhetoric of Ida B. Wells." *Reclaiming Rhetorica: Women in the Rhetorical Tradition*. Ed. Andrea A. Lunsford. Pittsburgh: U of Pittsburgh P, 1995.

———. "When the First Voice You Hear Is Not Your Own." *College Composition and Communication* 47 (1996): 29–40.

Russell, David. *Writing in the Academic Disciplines, 1870–1990: A Curricular History*. Carbondale: Southern Illinois UP, 1991.

Schutz, Aaron, and Anne Ruggles Gere. "Service Learning and English Studies: Rethinking 'Public' Service." *College English* 60.2 (1998): 129–49.

Scott, Fred Newton, and Joseph Villers Denney. *Composition-Literature*. Chicago: Allyn, 1902.

Shadduck, Glen. Autobiography. Box 44, Folder 15. Brookwood Labor College Collection. Archives of Labor and Urban Affairs, Wayne State U, Detroit.

Shoemaker, J. W. *Practical Elocution; for Use in Colleges and Schools and by Private Students*. Philadelphia: Penn, 1913.

Smith, Mortimer. *And Madly Teach: A Layman Looks at Public School Education*. Chicago: Regnery, 1949.

Smitherman, Geneva. "CCCC's Role in the Struggle for Language Rights." *College Composition and Communication* 50 (1999): 349–76.

———. *Talkin' and Testifyin': The Language of Black America*. Detroit: Wayne State UP, 1977.

Smitherman, Geneva, and Sylvia Cunningham. "Moving Beyond Resistance: Ebonics and African American Youth." *Journal of Black Psychology* 23.3 (1997): 227–32.

Solomon, Barbara Miller. *In the Company of Educated Women: A History of Women and Higher Education in America*. New Haven: Yale UP, 1985.

Spacks, Patricia Meyer, ed. *Advocacy in the Classroom: Problems and Possibilities*. New York: St. Martin's, 1996.

Statement of Purpose for Brookwood. 1921. Box 12, Folder 13. Brookwood Labor College Collection. Archives of Labor and Urban Affairs, Detroit.

Stuckey, J. Elspeth. *The Violence of Literacy*. Portsmouth: Boynton, 1991.

Stuckey, Sterling. *Slave Culture: Nationalist Theory and the Foundations of Black America*. New York: Oxford UP, 1987.

Tannen, Deborah. *You Just Don't Understand: Women and Men in Conversation*. New York: Ballantine, 1990.

Tildsley, Jane Watters. Letter to Mary Augusta Jordan. "A Tribute of 40 Years."

"A Tribute of 40 Years." Box 1, Folder 12. Smith College Archives, Northampton.

Twelfth Anniversary Review. Box 44, Folder 14. Brookwood Labor College Collection. Archives of Labor and Urban Affairs, Wayne State U, Detroit.

Varnum, Robin. *Fencing with Words: A History of Writing Instruction at Amherst College During the Era of Theodore Baird, 1938–1966.* Urbana: NCTE, 1996.

Wagner, Joanne. "'Intelligent Members or Restless Disturbers': Women's Rhetorical Styles, 1880–1920." *Reclaiming Rhetorica: Women in the Rhetorical Tradition.* Andrea A. Lunsford, ed. Pittsburgh: U of Pittsburgh P, 1995.

Walker, Alice, ed. *I Love Myself When I Am Laughing . . . and Then Again When I Am Looking Mean and Impressive: A Zora Neale Hurston Reader.* Old Westbury: Feminist, 1979.

Walker, Marion Sinclair. Letter to Mary Augusta Jordan. *A Tribute of 40 Years.*

Wallace, Janet. Course notes. Smith College Archives, Northampton.

Washington, Mary Helen. "Zora Neale Hurston: A Women Half in Shadow." Walker, Alice, 7–25.

Weltner, Barbara. "The Cult of True Womanhood: 1820–1860." *American Quarterly* 18 (1966): 158–74.

Wendell, Barrett. *English Composition.* New York: Scribner, 1891.

Wertheimer, Molly, ed. *Listening to Their Voices: The Rhetorical Activities of Historical Women.* Columbia: U of South Carolina P, 1997.

Wesley, Charles Harris. *The History of the National Association of Colored Women's Clubs: A Legacy of Service.* Washington: National Association of Colored Women's Clubs, 1984.

West, Cornel. "The New Cultural Politics of Difference." *Out There: Marginalization and Contemporary Cultures.* Ed. Russell Ferguson et al. Cambridge: MIT P, 1990. 19–36.

Whately, Richard. *Elements of Rhetoric.* 1846. Delmar: Scholars' Facsimiles and Reprints, 1991.

White, Hayden. "Interpretation in History." *Tropics of Discourse.* Baltimore: Johns Hopkins UP, 1978. 51–80.

The Wilberforce Alumnal. Wilberforce: Wilberforce U, 1885.

Wilbor, Elsie M., ed. *Delsarte Recitation Book.* New York: Werner, 1905.

Wilkins, Josephine. Letter to her sister. 1890. Smith College Archives, Northampton.

Wolfe, Alan. "She Just Doesn't Understand." *New Republic* 12 Dec. 1994: 26+.

Wolfram, Walt. "Language Ideology and Dialect: Understanding the Oakland Ebonics Controversy." *Journal of English Linguistics* 26 (1998): 108–21.

Wolters, Raymond. *The New Negro on Campus: Black College Rebellions of the 1920s.* Princeton: Princeton UP, 1975.

Woodson, Carter Godwin. *The Mis-Education of the Negro.* 1933. Trenton: Africa World, 1990.

Index

activism (*see also* labor movement): education for, 13, 62, 81–82; pedagogy of, 1–2, 28–29, 44–45; by teachers, 30, 46, 56–58

Addams, Jane, 50

Advocacy in the Classroom: Problems and Possibilities (Spacks), 20

AFL. *See* American Federation of Labor

African Americans (*see also* Brown, Hallie Quinn; multiculturalism; National Association of Colored Women; racism; Wilberforce University): Ebonics and, 20–21, 100, 103–4, 108–12; higher education of, 5–6, 11–12, 93, 135n. 4; history of, 5–6, 23, 61, 65–69; intelligence prejudice against, 2, 6, 20, 135n. 1; slavery of, 55, 61, 65–66, 67, 119; social responsibility and, 18–19, 62, 69–74; vernacular of, historically, 9, 14, 16, 61–65, 127

African Methodist Episcopal Church, 56, 71

Allen, Annie Ware Winsor, 42

Allen University, 57

Altenbaugh, Richard: on Brookwood, 80, 81, 84, 94; on workers' education movement, 76, 136n. 5, 139n. 2 (chap. 4)

American Federation of Labor (AFL), 93, 94–95, 138n. 1, 139n. 2 (chap. 4)

American Medicine, 6

Amherst College, 135n. 6

And Madly Teach (Smith), 139n. 4

Ann Arbor, Michigan, 103–4

Anzaldúa, Gloria, 24–25, 26, 125

"Apples" (in *Bits and Odds*), 63–64

Aristotle, 41, 82, 118

Aronowitz, Stanley, 17

assignments to students: at Amherst, 136n. 6; at Brookwood, 77–78, 83, 86–90; critical consciousness promoted by, 16–17, 99–100, 115–17, 118–19; politicization of, 1–2, 9–10, 13–14; service encouraged by, 19, 91–92, 124; at Smith, 28, 44–45, 47, 49

"As the Mantle Falls" (Brown), 56

Atlantic Monthly, 14, 28

Bahri, Deepika, 139n. 1

Baker, George H., 61, 66, 74

Ball, Arnetha, 104

Barnard College, 4, 46

Bartholomae, David, 105, 109

Bean, Robert Bennett, 6

Beauty Through Hygiene (Women's Home Library Series), 32

Bell, Alexander Melville, 58, 60

Bell, Bernard Iddings, 139n. 4

Bell Curve, The (Hernstein and Murray), 20

Bell's Standard Elocutionist (Bell and Bell), 67

Berlin, James, 21–22, 85–86, 88, 137n. 6, 139n. 3

Bernstein, Basil, 103

Bernstein, Irving, 7, 138n. 1

Biographical Dictionary of American Labor Leaders, 95

biology. *See* intelligence prejudice

Stuckey, J. Elspeth, 140n. 4
Stuckey, Sterling, 135n. 4
Students' Right to Their Own Language
    resolution (Conference on College Com-
    position and Communication), 102,
    104–5
suffrage. *See* voting

*Talkin' and Testifyin': The Language of Black
    America* (Smitherman), 103, 111
Tannen, Deborah, 106–7, 112
Tarr, Elvira, 136n. 5
Taylor, Warner, 86
"Teaching Language in Open Admissions"
    (Rich), 102
"Teaching of English, The" (Jordan), 29
Tennyson, Alfred, 64
Terrell, Mary Church, 57
Texas Monthly, 116
Thoreau, Henry David, 18
Thorndike, Edward, 22, 85
Tildsley, Jane Watters, 44
Till-Retz, Roberta, 112
"To Call a Thing by Its True Name: The Rhet-
    oric of Ida B. Wells" (Royster), 138n. 5
"Tribute of 40 Years, A" (to Jordan), 43
Trimbur, John, 115
Tuskegee Institute, 57
Twelfth Anniversary Review (Brookwood
    Labor College), 92–93, 95–96

unions. *See* labor movement
universality (*see also* standardization of lan-
    guage): diversity and, 22–23, 85–86,
    130; gender and, 59–60, 107, 112; race
    and, 54, 59–60
University of Minnesota, 112–13
University of Texas, 115–16, 120

Varnum, Robin, 9, 136n. 6
Vassar College, 4, 29, 46
vernacular (*see also* Ebonics): of African
    Americans, 9, 14, 16, 20, 61–65; avoid-
    ance of, 9, 20, 139n. 3; class and, 16, 77–
    78, 82–86, 113–14; culture and, 102–3
Violence of Literacy, The (Stuckey, J. E.),
    140n. 4

vocational training, 5–6, 135n. 4
Vorse, Mary Heaton, 87
voting: by African Americans, 5; by women,
    17, 28, 45–47, 126

Wagner, Joanne, 43
Walker, John, 58
Walker, Marion Sinclair, 43, 44
Wallace, Janet, 41
Washington, Booker T., 56–57, 135n. 4
Washington, Mary Helen, 64, 138n. 6
Ways with Words (Heath), 140n. 4
*"We Are Coming": The Persuasive Discourse
    of Nineteenth-Century Black Women* (Lo-
    gan), 138n. 5
Wellesley College, 4, 46
Wells, Ida B., 57, 138n. 5
Wendell, Barrett: influence of, 27, 31, 32–
    33, 40, 46; on language standards, 38–
    39, 137n. 6
Wesley, Charles Harris, 55, 137n. 2
West, Cornel, 67–68, 74
Whately, Richard, 41–42, 43
White, Emily, 4
White, Hayden, 97, 98, 128, 131
Whitecar, Robert, 87
Wilberforce Alumnal, 11–12
Wilberforce University (*see also* Brown,
    Hallie Quinn): Brown at, 14, 54, 56, 57;
    history of, 127, 136n. 8; mission state-
    ment of, 11–12
Wilkins, Josephine, 45
Willard, Frances, 50
Williams, Fannie Barrier, 57, 138n. 5
Wilson, Joseph, 136n. 5
Wisconsin School for Women Workers, 75
Wolfe, Alan, 106–7, 112, 121
Woll, Matthew, 95
Wolters, Raymond, 5–6
women (*see also* clubs, women's; feminism;
    Jordan, Mary Augusta; separatism; Smith
    College): critical consciousness of, 23–
    24, 41–46, 47–50, 52, 118; economics
    and, 3, 11, 49–50, 50, 123; education of,
    3–5, 45, 48, 135n. 2, 136n. 4; intelli-
    gence prejudice against, 2, 24; language
    standards and, 15–16, 106–8; Seven Sis-

Susan Kates is an assistant professor of English and women's studies at the University of Oklahoma, where she teaches in the composition, rhetoric, and literacy program. Her essays have appeared in *College English* and *College Composition and Communication*.